MONEY SKILLS FOR TEENS AND YOUNG ADULTS

8 Simple Ways to Manage Money, Start a Side-Hustle, Create a Positive Financial Mindset & Learn Lit Money-Making & Job-hunting Ideas

CAT MCCARTHY

Publishers Note

This publication is designed to provide accurate and authoritative information in regard to the subject matter covered. It is sold with the understanding that the publisher, author, editor, or any other involved in the preparation of this publication does not render psychological, financial, legal, or other professional services and is not responsible for any errors or omissions or the results obtained from the use of this publication. If expert assistance is needed, the services of a licensed professional should be sought.

Copyright © 2024 by Evolve Media Books

All rights reserved.

The content contained within this book may not be reproduced, duplicated, or transmitted without direct written permission from the publisher.

*This book is dedicated to you kids!
My grown ones and their teenagers whose love a support made this b[ook]
come to life. A special thank you to Kat and Cash, your perspective m[ade]
all the difference!
Love, Neema*

Contents

Introduction	9
1. MIND OVER MONEY	13
Power Up Your Money Mindset	14
What Is Mindset?	14
How Does Mindset Shape Our Money Decisions?	15
Inheriting Money Beliefs	22
Contrasting Money Beliefs	23
2. KICKSTART YOUR CASH FLOW	29
Unlocking Valuable Life Skills Through Employment	30
Landing a Job	33
Creating a Resume	34
Networking	35
Making a Job Wish List	35
Preparing for Interviews	36
Understanding your Paycheck	40
3. TURNING CLICKS INTO COINS	45
Turn Passion into Profit	46
Cashing in on Creativity	47
The Internet: Your Business Partner	48
Exciting Side Hustles That Make Money	49
Dean's Journey: From Creative Hobby to Thriving Business	55
Interactive Element: Dream Clouds Worksheet	59
Interactive Element: Branding Brainstorm	60
4. BANKING BEYOND THE BASICS	63
How Does Banking Work?	64
The Features of a Savings Account	65
The Basics of a Checking Account	67
Interactive Element: Savings vs. Checking Showdown	69
Strategy Power Up: Bank on Technology	71

Money Management Checklist — 73
Reality Check: A Lesson in Hidden Fees — 74
Sofia's Digital Piggy Bank — 75
Interactive Element: Mastering Money Management — 76
It All Goes Back to Mindset! — 79

5. **THE SAVING AND SPENDING BLUEPRINT** — 83
   Mastering Cash Flow — 84
   Interactive Element: Cash Flow Showdown — 86
   Future-Focused Budgeting — 87
   Interactive Element: Your Budget, Your Way — 89
   Save with Purpose — 91
   Set Savings Goals — 92
   Interactive Activity: Mapping Your Financial Dreams — 93
   Understanding Your Purchases — 95
   The Art of Smart Spending — 97
   Interactive Element: Spending Self-Check Worksheet — 98

6. **THE CREDIT CODE** — 101
   What is Credit? — 102
   The Cost of Using Credit — 103
   The Truth About Credit Cards — 104
   Your Credit Score — 106
   Interactive Element: The Tale of Two Approaches — 107
   Mastering Student Credit Cards — 109
   Interactive Element: Credit Card Tips and Commandments — 111
   From Credit Cards to Loans — 113
   Investing in Yourself With Loans — 114
   The Reality of Loans — 116

7. **SMALL STEPS TOWARD INVESTING FOR BIG REWARDS** — 119
   The Power of Starting Early — 121
   Interactive Element: Predicting Growth — 122
   Understanding Risks — 125
   Choosing the Right Investment Vehicle — 126
   Interactive Element: Your Micro-Investment Journey — 132

8. UNLOCKING THE FUTURE ... 135
   Dreams vs. Goals ... 136
   Interactive Element: Finding Help with Planning Your Future ... 137
   Mapping Out Your Goals ... 138
   Transforming Dreams into SMART Goals ... 141
   Interactive Element: Dream to SMART Goal Converter ... 144

   Conclusion ... 151
   Resources ... 155
   References ... 159

FREE GIFT!

Level Up Your Money Skills by creating a Positive Mindset

GET YOUR FREE COPY OF POWER THOUGHTS TODAY!

Introduction

Have you ever been stuck in class, wondering why the teacher keeps droning on and on about the importance of learning lessons for real life when you'd much rather find all you need to know on TikTok? Or, more specifically, why does your school's curriculum rarely touch on the topic of financial strategy, as if money is some big secret that needs to be locked away in a big treasure chest? That's a good one for TikTok, too!

In reality, while the internet and social media are great for finding tips and tricks, this world's information and misinformation are often mixed together so cleverly that it is difficult to discern the truth. What you need is a sound and reliable GPS about money that will lead you in the right direction toward financial success.

Consider this book as your navigational tool that will help you understand how to make your money work for you! As you follow the map that is carefully laid out in the following pages, you will begin to unlock the treasure chest and realize that your hopes and dreams for life are not as far off as you originally thought.

Whether you are just starting on your financial path or looking for a helpful refresher with the plain facts about money maneuvers, we're about to embark on this adventure together. Together, we'll eagerly explore the valuable treasures of knowledge, charting a course toward a future filled with endless possibilities. You will discover that building wealth is a process that begins with a positive outlook and continues by applying smart strategies to your finances.

What kind of strategies might you need to learn? We'll delve into the basics of banking, consider the art of saving alongside smart spending, and learn the essentials of budgeting in order to build long-term wealth. You'll consider the benefit of obtaining a traditional job in comparison with the excitement of developing as an entrepreneur and starting your own online gig. From there, since your ultimate goal is financial freedom, we will address the importance of setting mindful goals and explain the specific steps necessary to turn your dreams into a realistic action plan.

As we go through each of the strategies laid out in this book, you will meet real-life characters who are eager to take their own financial journeys and bring their own dreams to life. Young people like Maya, Dean, Sofia, and Mateo each have their own plan when it comes to money and will do whatever it takes to learn how to implement both their short-term and long-term goals. When they experience exhilarating successes, they celebrate those wins! When they face disappointment and failure, they see it as a learning opportunity to dust themselves off, refresh their minds on the knowledge they need, and dive back into the adventure once more.

Reading about the exploits of others, however, is only part of the excitement. The learning process is not just about reading and watching – it's also about doing! Every chapter includes several interactive sections for you to put the lesson into practice so that you will be well prepared for action when you are ready to implement the financial step in real life. As you complete each section, see it as much more than a successful lesson learned – it is an opportunity to envision how you will use the keys of financial success in your future!

As we head into our adventure ahead, feel free to bring others along on your journey. Whether you are requesting input and advice from a trusted adult or brainstorming with a peer, having someone join you for each financial step means that the valuable lessons will multiply to create an even greater profit.

Are you ready for the financial adventure of a lifetime? Let's unlock the treasure chest!

1

Mind Over Money

 "The mind is everything. What you think, you become."

Buddha

There once was a great elephant, known worldwide as a symbol of strength and might, but tethered by its owner to a small stake with a tiny rope. A young boy, seeing the gigantic animal held captive in this manner, was curious why the huge animal did not break free. The owner explained: When the elephant was young, it was bound by a strong rope that prevented its escape. As it grew, the elephant continued to believe that the rope was strong, even when it could have easily snapped the frayed old rope as a colossal adult.

This fable lives on as a testimony to the immense influence that our thoughts and beliefs hold over our lives. Like that elephant, we can sometimes limit ourselves, allowing tiny ropes of doubt and fear to hold us back from our true potential.

"Money is a tool; it will take you wherever you wish, but it will not replace you as the driver."

Ayn Rand

Power Up Your Money Mindset

As we embark on our journey of learning how to practically manage money, we must start by recognizing that everything begins in our minds. Think of your mindset as the rudder of a ship that guides the direction in which you sail. In other words, the way you think about money will shape your financial reality!

Another way to consider it is that your mind is the true hidden treasure! Perhaps it is currently a diamond in the rough, but the good news is that you already possess it and can learn to use it in powerful ways to gain wealth, happiness, and endless possibilities for the rest of your life. This is the beginning of your financial future, so let's open the treasure chest!

What Is Mindset?

Your mindset is the operating system of your brain or the lens through which you view the world around you. It is a collection of your thoughts, beliefs, and attitudes that influence how you perceive reality. While everyone has their own mindset, there are two main kinds that people fall into: the fixed mindset and the growth mindset.

Fixed Mindset: If you have a fixed mindset, you tend to believe that your abilities, intelligence, and personal qualities are set in stone. When faced with a challenge, you might feel afraid of failure and try to avoid the situation instead of going through the process of learning from your mistakes. In those situations, you feel like any extra exertion is unproductive, and you would rather spend energy doing something where you are guaranteed to succeed.

Growth Mindset: By comparison, if you have a growth mindset, you believe that your abilities and intelligence can flourish through dedication, focused attention, and learning how to succeed! You will eagerly embrace challenges and persevere through setbacks instead of avoiding these situations, seeing them as great opportunities for learning and growth. While this type of mindset is not as common to cultivate, consider how you can develop this attitude and expand your life's possibilities!

How Does Mindset Shape Our Money Decisions?

You might ask, "What does that have to do with money?" Well, your mindset about finances is a specific part of your overall mindset about life, shaping your beliefs about money, wealth, and financial success. To further illustrate this concept, let's dive into the stories of Maya and Sofia, two individuals whose mindsets greatly influence their spending habits.

Maya's Money Mindset: Meet Maya, a clever 16-year-old who knows how to make her money work for her. Ever since she was 12, she babysat her younger sister and housesat for a neighbor when they went on vacation. Those gigs bring in a little cash here and there, and it all adds up.

To make Maya's story special, she always has had a savvy approach and positive attitude to money. Instead of spending her hard-earned cash right away, she saves it toward her future dreams—being independent, having her own place, making her own decisions, and building a happy life for herself. She is grateful for her opportunities and proud of herself.

Every time she earns money from babysitting or housesitting, Maya puts a certain portion into a savings account. Occasionally, she spends a little on fun things or new clothes, but most of the time she focuses on her goals. Her even bigger dream is to learn how to invest her money and watch it grow. She knows that every dollar she earns has the potential to turn into something bigger and more amazing!

Sofia Steps Up: Now let's meet Sofia, an artistic 18-year-old who is passionate about crafting unique jewelry. Sofia's family has the rule that financial safety comes from job security, or holding a traditional job with a steady paycheck. But Sofia wants her creativity and passion for making jewelry to be her ticket to financial success. She knows that her mindset shapes her actions and plans to create her own money journey.

Even though her family isn't confident about her plan, Sofia starts making jewelry to sell at school and to friends and family. Although she doesn't make much money at first, she doesn't get discouraged because she understands that building something awesome takes time and effort.

We will follow Sofia's story throughout this book, watching her ups and downs as she works to create her own business. The most important thing in her journey is that Sofia's unique money mindset teaches her over time that having a different outlook than her family is perfectly okay! As she continues to believe in herself and take actions that match her passion, Sofia learns that having her own money mindset leads to success in a unique way.

"Your mindset is the compass that guides your financial journey. Make sure it points towards abundance and prosperity."

Maya and Sofia's stories show us that mindset is a powerful force in shaping how we manage our finances. Whether it's the responsible pursuit of saving money in Maya's case or the entrepreneurial drive and willingness to take chances in Sofia's case, mindset can significantly impact our actions!

Before we dive deeper into exploring how various mindsets can affect your financial choices, let's pause and do some self-reflection in the quiz below about our tendencies to spend, save, give, or invest our hard-earned money.

Interactive Element: Money Mindset Quiz

Instructions: Answer each question honestly to figure out your current money mindset. It's like finding your treasure map; knowing where you are right now will help you navigate to where you want to be!

1. When you receive money (e.g., allowance, gift), what's the first thing you think of doing?

    A. Spend it on something fun.
    B. Save it for later.
    C. Give it to someone in need.
    D. Invest it for future goals.

2. Imagine you won $500 in a contest. What would you most likely do with it?

   A. Spend it all on shopping, entertainment, or a new gadget.
   B. Save a portion and spend the rest.
   C. Donate some to a charity and save the rest.
   D. Save it all for future financial goals.

3. How do you feel when you hear about someone else's financial success (e.g., a friend starting a profitable business)?

   A. Jealous or envious.
   B. Happy for them but wondering if you could achieve the same.
   C. Inspired and motivated to work toward your own financial goals.
   D. Eager to learn from their success and replicate it.

4. Your parents offer to match every dollar you save from your allowance with an extra dollar. What's your reaction?

   A. Not interested; you'd rather spend it all now.
   B. You might save a little to get some extra money later.
   C. Excited; you see it as a chance to save now and treat a friend later.
   D. Thrilled; you view it as an opportunity to build wealth over time.

5. You receive your first paycheck from your part-time job. What's the first thing you think about doing with the money?

   A. Splurging on something you've wanted for a while.
   B. Putting some aside for future expenses or savings.

C. Donating a portion to a cause you care about.
D. Planning how to invest and grow your money.

6. Your friends invite you on an unplanned, expensive weekend trip. How do you respond?

A. Join the trip immediately, even if it means stretching your budget.
B. Check your budget to see if you can afford it without impacting your savings.
C. Suggest ways to make the trip more affordable or find budget-friendly alternatives.
D. Politely decline the invitation, explaining your commitment to your financial goals.

7. You discover a valuable item while cleaning your room, but you're unsure if it's worth anything. What's your next step?

A. Sell it online or at a garage sale to make some extra cash.
B. Research its value and decide whether to keep, sell, or save it.
C. Give it to a friend or donate it to a charity.
D. Consult with an expert to appraise it and consider long-term investment options.

8. Your favorite online store has a big sale, but you hadn't planned to buy anything. How do you react?

A. Jump at the chance to score some great deals, even if it means going beyond your budget.
B. Browse the sale items but only purchase if they align with your planned expenses.

C. Consider purchasing a treat, as long as it doesn't compromise your savings or giving goals.

D. Resist the temptation to buy, reminding yourself of your long-term financial objectives.

Your Current Mindset is…

Mostly A's: Spender Money Mindset

You enjoy spending money on immediate pleasures like Sarah, a 17-year-old who is passionate about fashion. She's known for her spontaneous shopping sprees and always staying up to date with the latest trends. When Sarah receives extra cash, she can't help but imagine all the fun she can have. Concert tickets, stylish clothes, and dining out with friends are at the top of her list. Sarah's motto is, "Why wait when you can enjoy life now?" While Sarah's enthusiasm is infectious, she sometimes wonders if there's more to her money than fleeting moments of excitement. If you can relate to Sarah, this book can help you find a balance between living in the moment and securing your financial future.

Mostly B's: Saver Money Mindset

You're cautious with money and tend to save for the future like Alex, a 15-year-old high school student who has always been financially savvy. When he won $500 in a contest, he decided to save a portion for a savings goal and future plans. He understands the importance of saving money for his future financial well-being, even when tempted by short-term spending. Alex values financial stability and believes in the power of saving for building wealth. He knows that saving is the first step towards achieving his long-term goals. If you can relate to Alex, this book will help you explore new ways to grow your savings and achieve even greater financial security.

Mostly C's: Giver Money Mindset

You are often described as compassionate and enjoy helping others like Emily, a 16-year-old with a heart of gold. Whenever she hears about someone else's financial success, she feels inspired and motivated to work toward her own goals. She's an active volunteer and regularly donates to various charitable causes. Emily believes that financial success is not just about personal wealth but also about positively impacting the world. She's excited to continue her journey of generosity and wants to learn how to create a structured plan for her giving. If you can relate to Emily, this book will help you develop a strategy for your charitable endeavors while ensuring your financial well-being.

Mostly D's: Planner Money Mindset

You tend to focus on long-term financial goals and future security, like James, a 14-year-old whose mom is a CPA and has helped him create the ultimate financial plan. He believes every dollar saved and invested today is a building block for a secure future. When his mom offers to match his savings, he is thrilled, seeing it as an opportunity to accelerate his wealth-building journey. James focuses on long-term financial goals and diligently plans for his personal and financial future. He knows that he can achieve his dreams and aspirations with careful preparation. If you can relate to James, this book will be a valuable resource for further developing your financial plan and securing the future you've been diligently working toward.

 "I am in control of my financial destiny, and I choose to think and act like a wealth creator."

Inheriting Money Beliefs

Guess what? You've inherited more than just your family's weird holiday traditions or secret recipes. As Sofia learns, the views that your parents, guardians, or teachers have about money are also passed down to you. Let's think about how this specifically plays out in the lives of the characters that we previously met.

Scenario 1: The Money Worrier. While Alex is a great saver, his parents were always stressing about bills and living paycheck to paycheck as he grew up. Money was always a topic of worry at home and Alex watched his parents worry constantly about money because it appeared scarce and hard to get. As a result, Alex constantly stresses about money and making financial choices in fear.

Scenario 2: The Money Wizard. On the flip side, Emily's parents were money wizards. Emily picked up these financial superpowers from her family. She's got a positive money mindset, believing in the power of saving and investing for her future, while still having enough to share. Emily sees money as a tool to help her level up.

These stories highlight how your family's money beliefs can rub off on you. Remember that your beliefs aren't set in stone! Your family's past money story does not decide your financial journey since you have the power to challenge and transform any belief.

"The only limits on your income are the limits you set in your mind."

Thomas S. Manson

Contrasting Money Beliefs

Now, let's take a look at common money ideas that might hold you back, giving you a beggar's belief. In comparison, think about how the millionaire's mindset welcomes in opportunities and takes you places!

Begger's Belief: "Money is hard to find."

Millionaire's Mindset: "Money is all around me."

If you have the mindset of a beggar, you believe that discovering money is as rare as finding a unicorn! Instead, the millionaire knows that money-making opportunities are everywhere and actively looks for ways to grow earnings and explore new financial avenues.

Beggar's Belief: "I can't control if I become wealthy or not."

Millionaire's Mindset: "I am in control of my financial destiny."

Some people believe that their financial future is decided by their family's situation and other factors, resulting in feelings of helplessness and lack of motivation. To be like a millionaire, however, you must face financial obstacles with determination! Your financial journey can be a path you design and build, taking you where you want to go.

Beggar's Belief: "Money can't buy me happiness."

Millionaire's Mindset: "Money enhances my quality of life."

While money alone cannot guarantee happiness, it can provide opportunities and experiences that contribute to a fulfilling life. A millionaire understands that financial well-being can positively impact overall well-being.

Beggar's Belief: "I never have any extra money."

Millionaire's Mindset: "I always find opportunities to save and invest."

A scarcity mindset often leads to the belief that there's never enough money left after expenses. A millionaire seeks to be grateful for what you have and uses opportunities to save, invest, and grow wealth.

Holding onto the belief of a beggar is like carrying heavy weights that slow down your progress and limit your potential. When you let go of these beliefs, the weights fall off your shoulders and give you the freedom to run toward a future full of exciting opportunities!

"I release old money stories and unhelpful beliefs that lead me in the opposite direction of where I want to go, making space for a wealth-conscious mindset."

Rewriting Old Stories

Now that we have the awareness to overturn limiting money beliefs, it's time to rewrite your old money narrative! Think of it as picking up a pen and composing a new chapter in your financial story. As an example, let's look at how two famous people used a positive mindset to turn their obstacles into success stories!

Bruno Mars: From Humble Beginnings to Musical Stardom

You might know him as the multi-talented singer, songwriter, and producer Bruno Mars, but did you know about his challenging childhood? Born in Honolulu, Hawaii, as Peter Gene Hernandez, he grew up with his family in a one-bedroom apartment and faced many hardships. However, this adversity didn't deter him. In an interview with "60 Minutes," Bruno Mars revealed that his background helped instill a sense of determination to succeed as a recording artist in Hollywood. He said, "Maybe that's why I have this mentality—I know I'm going to figure it out, just give me some time." His journey reminds us that a challenging financial background doesn't define our potential for success. With determination, talent, and the right mindset, he achieved remarkable heights in the music industry.

J.K. Rowling: A Tale of Perseverance and Imagination

The beloved author of the *Harry Potter* series, J.K. Rowling is no stranger to financial hardship. Before her books became a global phenomenon, her life was far from glamorous as a single mother living on welfare. She struggled to make ends meet while pursuing her dream of writing. Yet, her unwavering determination and creativity led her to create a magical world that captivated millions of readers. J.K. Rowling's story is a testament to the power of imagination, resilience, and belief in oneself. She transformed her life from a financial struggle to becoming one of the world's most prosperous and beloved authors.

"The future depends on what you do today."

Mahatma Gandhi

Interactive Element: Give Thanks

Sometimes, old money beliefs can make you feel like you're always missing out or that you'll never have enough. But there is an unexpected superpower that can transform your thoughts and feelings—gratitude! Gratitude is a game-changer that can flip your perspective from thinking about what you lack to recognizing what you've got in abundance. It helps you tune out the bad and tune into the good. When you practice gratitude, it's like a reminder of all the cool stuff you're thankful for, and it can help you see money and everything else through a more positive lens.

Here's how it works: Use these gratitude prompts to start appreciating the good stuff in your life. In turn, as you shift your focus from what's missing to what's already there, you will face life with a more positive attitude, further motivating you to pursue your dreams! Spend some time digging into these questions with an open heart and a thoughtful mind.

Gratitude Prompts:

1. People You Appreciate: Who makes a difference in your life, and why?
2. Your Well-Being: What makes you feel good, physically and mentally?
3. Memorable Moments: Share a memory that brings joy and why it's special.
4. Your Talents: List unique skills you have and how they've positively impacted you.
5. Nature's Wonders: What aspects of nature or your surroundings make you smile?
6. Everyday Comforts: Which daily items bring you comfort or happiness?

7. Growth Through Challenges: What did a tough experience teach you? How did it help you grow?
8. Future Hopes: What are some opportunities you're thankful for? What dreams do you look forward to?
9. Kindness Received: Note some acts of kindness you've encountered and why they matter.
10. Self-Appreciation: What do you love about yourself that makes you unique?

Remember, there are no right or wrong answers to these prompts. Your gratitude journey is personal, so the thing that matters most is that you're sincere. Take your time with these prompts, practice gratitude often, and embrace the power of gratitude to transform your money mindset and enhance your overall well-being.

What's Your Story?

While you are on this life-changing journey, it is important to stop and ask yourself, What is the money narrative that you want to tell? Is an old mindset holding you back, or do you have a new story filled with positivity, growth, and financial abundance? Armed with the knowledge in this chapter, it's your turn to step onto the stage and rewrite the parts of your story that you want to change. If you recognize limiting beliefs, challenge them and replace them with thoughts of success, abundance, and possibility.

More importantly, answer this: How can your new money mindset motivate you to put concrete actions into play that will jumpstart your financial future? Part of the answer is found in the next chapter, where we explore practical steps to earn money and confidently navigate the job world. Are you ready to take the next step toward financial empowerment?

2

Kickstart Your Cash Flow

 "Nothing will work unless you do."

Maya Angelou

Clara was frustrated. She wanted to buy a tablet to help her organize her high school schedule in real-time, but she just didn't have enough money. Plus, summer was coming up, she was planning to be a part of the local theater, and she knew it would be really helpful to keep track of her growing list of responsibilities.

When Clara went to talk to her mom about it, Grammy was listening from the other room.

"I'm halfway there, but I can't just keep waiting and waiting for my allowance, and I'm just not sure what to do next!"

Suddenly, Grammy's voice piped up from the living room, "Honey? Just get a job!"

Clara immediately felt frustrated by the simplistic answer, but as she thought about it, Grammy's advice seemed like a really good idea. Holding a job, even a part-time gig so it wouldn't cut into her busy performance calendar, would definitely give her the freedom to purchase a tablet of her very own!

As you will discover in this chapter, having a steady income gives you the ability to expand your wealth and work toward your greater financial goals. Let's explore practical ideas, strategies, and possibilities for finding and landing a job to kickstart your cash flow!

Unlocking Valuable Life Skills Through Employment

Earning money opens the door to life lessons and skills that stretch beyond the classroom. Remember Maya from the last chapter? Her first job supplied her with the essential tools to shape her into a confident and independent individual who knows how to grow her bank account!

Today, Maya still earns money by babysitting and housesitting, but she has bigger dreams. Her goal is to supplement her current income and gather practical experience that she can later apply to her future career.

After a few weeks of searching, she landed a part-time position at a local bookstore. Let's look at the skills and real-life lessons Maya acquired through her job and explore the valuable opportunities that a career can also provide for you.

Responsibility

Maya's first experience was in responsibility. She already knew the importance of responsibility from babysitting and housesitting, and it was one of the things her boss liked most about her when offering her the job. At the bookstore, Maya learned greater responsibility when showing up on time for her shifts, keeping the shelves well-organized, and assisting customers with their book selections.

Most of all, Maya learned that responsibility is not just a word or a concept but something to practice daily. By fulfilling her duties, she learns to be punctual and accountable. After all, her boss was hiring for the job because he really needed the help, and Maya does not want to disappoint her!

Looking to the future, Maya realizes that this skill is invaluable and is helping to mold her into in a reliable and trustworthy individual who can be depended upon even more. It gives her the confidence to manage her own life with skill.

Character

Next, Maya encounters experiences that can only be described as character-building. The bookstore regularly faces challenges from demanding customers to busy days with minimal staff. These experiences build Maya's character as she learns to be resilient, adaptable, and patient, providing her customers with a considerate, enjoyable, and efficient experience while she is continuously under pressure.

As Maya masters each challenge, she discovers that facing these situations head-on provides her with even greater opportunities for personal growth and resilience. For example, she knows if she is going to succeed, she will have to approach challenges with a smile. Each of these character-building scenarios increases her overall confidence, makes her more effective at diffusing tension, and gives her the capability to be kind and helpful under pressure.

Communication

Maya realizes she is developing new skills in communicating at work. She converses with colleagues, supervisors, and customers from different age groups, backgrounds, and preferences, enhancing her interpersonal communication skills.

These interactions show that she can return the encouragement she already received, communicating warmly and effectively while being a supportive team player. She begins to experience more confidence as her interpersonal skills empower her to navigate social situations easily, forging meaningful connections and fostering teamwork, which are priceless skills in all personal and business relationships.

Independence

The day finally arrives when Maya receives her first paycheck! Feeling great satisfaction, independence, and self-reliance, she immediately opens the envelope and deposits the balance into her online bank. Maya embraces the newfound freedom as she continues working and managing her growing bank balance. No longer solely reliant on her parents for financial support, she gains even more confidence and begins to make her own spending and saving decisions, paving the way for her financial freedom. She wastes no time practicing smart financial choices that support her plan for saving and investing for long-term financial stability and wealth.

Maya's confidence grows with each completed shift and every new challenge she overcomes. She realizes that she possesses the skills and determination to handle work-related tasks successfully. This newfound self-assurance isn't limited to her job but extends to every aspect of her life, making her more self-assured and capable of facing life's hard choices. The confidence instilled by these experiences allow Maya to tackle various financial decisions with a positive outlook, helping her balance her saving and spending to keep her financial goals on track.

Maya's story highlights the incredible rewards, personal growth, and skills gained through having a job. Securing employment and earning money is only the starting point, but it might be the most important one. It's the moment that you begin building a financial foundation for your future and become a person primed for success. Now, the door is open to other financial strategies like saving, investing, starting a business, running a side hustle, and making your money work for you! The financial habits and life skills you develop now will serve you well for a lifetime and will never fail to deliver rewards.

"Whether you think you can, or you think you can't – you're right."

Henry Ford

Landing a Job

Jorge was a freshman in high school when he applied for his first job at a frozen yogurt shop. He was excited but nervous about the upcoming interview. To overcome his anxiety, Jorge took proactive steps. He researched common interview questions, practiced his answers in front of a mirror, and even sought advice from his older sister.

When the big day arrived, he was still a little jittery, but his preparation gave him the confidence he needed. Jorge's enthusiasm and determination shone through during the interview, impressing the manager, who offered Jorge the job. He left the interview feeling proud that he had taken the preparation process seriously.

Jorge's story illustrates the exciting and life-changing experience of getting your first job. It's not just about the paycheck; it's your ticket to financial independence and personal growth! At the same time, stepping into the job market can be very intimidating, so we're here to help you navigate this new adventure. Here are some practical tips to help you land your first job and make a strong impression, just like Jorge did.

Creating a Resume

Drafting a resume might seem daunting if you have little job experience. But don't worry; starting with a simple one-page document is perfectly fine. List your full name, preferred name, address, and phone number at the top of the page.

Next, highlight your skills and any relevant coursework, certifications, extracurricular activities, or hobbies that led you to apply for this job in the first place. For instance, if you love to bake and apply for jobs at bakeries or coffee houses, they will love your enthusiasm!

Keep your resume clean and concise, and you will impress the interviewer! You can find many different kinds of online templates to make this process easier. See the resources page for an easy resume builder.

Networking

Remember that you are not alone in this journey! Connections you already have can lead to incredible opportunities. Talk to your family, friends, teachers, coaches, and neighbors for ideas and referrals since they might know about job openings or offer valuable advice. These people care about your success and may have more insights than you think.

Making a Job Wish List

When searching for your first job, thinking about what interests you is vital. Why would you want to work at a job that you don't enjoy? Here's how to create your job wish list:

1. **Identify Your Passions.** Consider what activities you look forward to doing or the topics that excite you. Do you love fashion, books, music, technology, sports, animals, art, or helping others?
2. **Find Like-Minded Businesses.** Think about stores in your community that align with your passions. It could be a local sporting goods outlet, clothing boutique, animal shelter, movie theater, art supply store, gallery or museum, or any place that shares your interests.
3. **Track Your Progress.** Make notes about the businesses or stores that you have on your job wish list. This list is a reminder of the next steps to take, and it's a powerful tool to guide your job search in the right direction.

"Opportunities don't happen; you create them."

Chris Grosser

Taking Action

Once you've identified the places you'd like to work and are close enough to where you live to get there on time, take action. Visit these places, express your interest, and ask if they have any job openings. Even if they don't currently have positions, representing your passion for their business can leave a lasting impression! You can also ask to leave a copy of your resume with the owner or hiring manager. Often, local businesses will have a website with their applications, so you can fill one out online before you stop in. This is a great way to have a foot in the door. When you arrive with your resume and let them know you have already completed the application, they are sure to be impressed!

Embracing Rejection

Only some job applications will result in an interview, and only some interviews will secure a job. Not getting a particular job is part of the process, so don't let that discourage you. Instead, realize that you are not the reason that you didn't get the job or the interview! In other words, your job is still out there, so it is time to get out there and find it!

Preparing for Interviews

Interviews can be intimidating, but with the proper preparation and mindset, you can be like Jorge and turn them into opportunities to shine. Before each interview, think about what activities you're into every day since these can be the reason you get the job.

Do you fix appliances around the house? Are you super creative? Can you paint or draw? Are you very organized? Are you a movie enthusiast? Are you the trusted neighborhood babysitter? Are you a skilled lacrosse player? All of your natural activities speak to your strengths and passions, making you a valuable employee in the place where you naturally fit. Interviews are your chance to shine and show potential employers why you're the perfect fit for their team.

Practice with these common interview questions:

"Can you tell me about yourself?"

This is a common opening question. Use this question to talk briefly about your background, your education, and what you're passionate about.

"Why do you want to work here?"

Consider what specifically attracted you to the company or job position. Was it the company's values or products? Did you see opportunities for personal growth or to help people?

"What are your strengths and weaknesses?"

This is a classic question to assess self-awareness. Focus on your strengths and explain how you've used them. When talking about your weaknesses, emphasize the importance of discussing how you work toward self-improvement.

Example of a Strength:

"One of my strengths is being a good listener and communicator. In my school's debate club, I've worked on developing these skills by actively listening to my teammates' arguments and responding with well-thought-out points. I've also had the opportunity to participate in public speaking events, which has improved my communication

abilities. So, my strong communication skills will be valuable in this role."

Example of a Weakness:

"One area I'm working on is time management. I sometimes feel overwhelmed by juggling school assignments, extracurricular activities, and personal projects. I've started using a planner and setting clear daily goals to address this. I've also been practicing breaking down tasks into smaller, manageable steps. I've noticed improvements and am committed to continuing my time management growth as I step into the professional world."

"What is a challenging situation you've faced?"

Use this question to talk about a time you've encountered a problem and how you solved it. This is your chance to reinforce your resilience and problem-solving skills.

Example:

"One challenging situation I faced was during a group project at school. Our team had to prepare a presentation within a tight deadline. Then we encountered a setback when our primary data source for the project fell through at the last minute. We were left with limited time to find an alternative.

"To tackle this challenge, I quickly regrouped with my team, and we decided to divide our efforts. While it was an intense couple of days with long hours of research and data collection, our determination and teamwork paid off. We compiled the required information and delivered a successful presentation on time. This experience reinforced my problem-solving skills and taught me the importance of teamwork in overcoming obstacles. It also showed me the value of staying calm under pressure and finding creative solutions when faced with unexpected challenges."

"Can you provide an example of when you worked as part of a team?"

This is an opportunity for you to showcase your teamwork and communication skills. Share a specific example that emphasizes your role in the team's success.

Example:

"I'd like to share a great experience during a community service project at my school. Our mission was to gather donations for a local shelter and host a community fair to shine a spotlight on the issue of homelessness. I took on the role of being the event coordinator, which meant that I was responsible for ensuring the fair went off without a hitch. I organized setting up booths, getting volunteers, and ensuring everything ran smoothly. We collected many donations, and many people attended the community fair. We all brought our special skills to the table and made a real impact. I learned that working together is super important, and when we do, we can make some cool things happen!"

It is also helpful when you prepare questions to ask your interviewer, too. For instance, ask about the store's most popular items or when the boutique tends to be the busiest. This shows your genuine interest in the position and demonstrates your eagerness to learn.

"Success is not final, failure is not fatal: It is the courage to continue that counts."

Winston Churchill

Dressing for Success

When preparing for an interview, consider the company's dress code. Selecting a casual, comfortable outfit that matches the company's style is a good choice. On the other hand, applying for an office job means you will want to select business attire to convey that you're an excellent fit for the work culture. First impressions matter, so make sure your outfit is appropriate for your desired job!

Displaying Confidence

Confidence is your secret weapon. Jorge's confidence during his interview was a game-changer, and it can be for you, too. Believe in yourself! Maintain eye contact, offer a firm handshake, and speak clearly. Even if you feel nervous, projecting confidence will make a positive impression. Smile! With the proper preparation and a positive attitude, you're on the path to success!

Understanding your Paycheck

You have finally landed your first job. Congratulations! Now let's fast-forward to the moment you have been waiting for—payday! There is no better feeling than earning your own money. Still, it's essential to consider an important piece of the puzzle: taxes. When you earn a paycheck, some of your hard-earned money may go to the government. While every country and region has their own regulations and ways of handling taxes, since Jorge lives in the United States, let's consider the American method of processing income as one example.

Let's get back to Jorge's story. After acing his job interview at the frozen yogurt shop and landing the gig, he was stoked. But after putting in his hours and receiving his first paycheck, he noticed his earnings were lower than expected. Jorge worked 27 hours at $9.00 per hour, so he expects to earn $243.00. Instead, he receives closer to $200.00. What happened?

Everyone earning money in the U.S. pays federal income tax, Social Security, and FICA. Most states also charge state income tax. All of these taxes are withheld directly from your wages, and your paycheck reflects that. Your *gross* income is what you earned before taxes, which would be Jorge's expected earnings of $243. But your *net* income is what you take home after paying mandatory things like income tax, Social Security, and FICA.

Let's break it down even further!

- **Gross Wages:** The total you earned before deductions.
- **YTD Gross:** A summary of all your earnings, deductions, and net pay from the start of the year to the current pay period (year to date).
- **Federal Tax:** Money set aside for federal income tax, deducted in each pay period to avoid a big tax bill when you file your return.
- **FICA Tax:** A portion your employer withholds to pay Social Security tax, which supports retired and disabled individuals. You and your employer both chip in.
- **FICA Medicare:** Money withheld for Medicare, a federal health insurance program mainly for those 65 and older or disabled.
- **State Tax:** Amount taken out by your employer to cover state income tax (not all states have this). This prevents a large one-time payment during tax season.
- **Net Pay:** What you take home, calculated by subtracting all the deductions. This is your actual "take-home" pay.

Interactive Element: Job Progress Checklist

Jorge's journey to landing his first job demonstrated the importance of preparation, confidence, and determination. Here's your chance to follow in his footsteps. Use this checklist to track your progress in landing your next job.

1. Create Your First Resume

    ☐ List your full name, preferred name, address, and phone number on your resume.
    ☐ Highlight your skills, coursework, certifications, extracurricular activities, or hobbies relevant to your desired job.
    ☐ Visit this resource to make your resume process easier! [link, QR code].

2. Start Networking

    ☐ Talk to family, friends, teachers, coaches, and neighbors for job openings or advice.
    ☐ Record the names of people you've spoken to and their recommendations.

3. Make a Job Wish List

    ☐ Identify your passions and interests, such as fashion, books, music, sports, art, etc.
    ☐ List local businesses or stores that align with your passions.
    ☐ Create your job wish list to guide your job search.

4. Take action

- Visit the businesses on your job wish list and inquire about job openings.
- Record the dates of your visits and the names of people you spoke to.
- Leave a copy of your resume where applicable.

5. Prepare for Interviews

- Think about your daily activities and strengths that make you a valuable employee.
- Practice answering common interview questions.
- Develop a list of questions to ask your interviewer to show your genuine interest.

6. Dress for Success

- Consider the company's dress code when selecting your interview outfit.
- Make sure your attire matches the desired job and the company's culture.

7. Confidence is Key

- Believe in yourself and maintain confidence during interviews.
- Practice maintaining eye contact, offering a solid handshake, and speaking clearly when meeting new people.
- Remember to smile, since confidence is your secret weapon.

Kickstarting Your Way to Success!

This chapter provided insights and strategies for earning money by working for someone else and keeping a job. This strategy is a tried and true way to kickstart your cash flow and lay the foundation for growing your financial goals. Earning money isn't just about the numbers in your bank account; it's your ticket to freedom, confidence, maturity, and wealth.

Now think about this: What if you could turn your own ideas and passions into profits? Well, it has never been easier to find ways to bring your interests into the marketplace and make money! In the next chapter, we'll take a look at the entrepreneurial spirit in action and get some inspiration on how side hustles allow you to make money, all while working for yourself and doing something that you love!

3

Turning Clicks into Coins

 "Your big opportunity may be right where you are now."

Napoleon Hill

The digital era has opened up a treasure trove of opportunities for everyone on the planet to be a businessperson, whether they own a computer, a tablet, or just a basic smartphone.

In this chapter, we'll dive into understanding how you can turn your creative ideas into a source of income right from the comfort of your own home. Perhaps you're eager to showcase your creative talents while bringing in some extra cash or hope to sell unique products on the vast online marketplace. Let's learn all about earning money online and the great potential of side hustles, all of which pave the way for a future where you call the shots and carve your own path to success!

Turn Passion into Profit

Remember Sofia from Chapter 1? She didn't just want to create jewelry; her ambition was to turn her talent into a successful business. Using her savings from babysitting gigs, she started investing in her future by purchasing jewelry-making supplies.

Sofia also needed more confidence to know how to transform her hobby into a real-life business. Recognizing the vast resources available to her, she turned to YouTube as her personal business school to gain expertise.

In the days and weeks that followed, Sofia absorbed valuable lessons about creating an online shop, establishing a brand, connecting with customers, and effectively marketing her goods. She then began harnessing the power of the Internet by opening an Instagram account, connecting with millions of potential clients, and handling inquiries about available pieces—just as custom orders started to roll in!

While running an online shop was challenging between school, friends, sports, and home life, Sofia diligently managed her time by dedicating certain hours to work on her venture. Her investment, both in time and money, paid off as her business continued to grow. Her marketing skills improved, and she fostered strong connections with her customers by inviting them to follow her on Instagram.

As the year progressed, Sofia expanded her business into a line of customized accessories that complemented her jewelry. She recognized the value of her unique creations and strategically increased those prices, further broadening her customer base. When she looked back from where she came, Sofia was proud of how her brand grew to include two thriving product lines that gave her financial success.

Cashing in on Creativity

Now let's meet Mateo, an 18-year-old gamer who wants to turn his passion into a profitable venture. He began his journey by creating the "GameMasterMateo" YouTube channel without touching his savings. Armed with just a gaming console that he received for his birthday, a computer that he swapped some work for, and free video editing software, he laid the foundation for his channel.

As Mateo recorded, edited, and shared his initial batch of videos, he also actively immersed himself in gaming communities. He collaborated with fellow gamers, brainstormed content ideas, and gleaned valuable insights as part of his routine. His video recording and editing skills showed noticeable improvement with each video he produced.

The exciting part was that he didn't have to wait long to see tangible results, thanks to the advertisements that generated earnings. Every time someone watched his video, a set of ads would roll, and the YouTube rewards would keep adding up.

Over time, Mateo discovered the audience that enjoyed his unique personality and style. As he focused on connecting with them, in just ten months, his channel crossed a remarkable milestone – 100,000 subscribers! His success didn't go unnoticed; gaming companies began approaching him with sponsorship offers!

Creating a YouTube channel brought its own set of challenges. Mateo quickly learned the importance of relying on a calendar to help him stay on track and balance different elements of his life. Online content creation also proved to be competitive and unpredictable, occasionally resulting in criticism and negative comments from viewers. Mateo relied on his growth mindset, developed a thick skin, and focused on the positive feedback and support from his growing community of subscribers to keep moving forward.

Mateo's efforts paid off big time with brand partnerships, as companies began paying him to promote their video games. YouTube's immediate ad earnings also helped him increase his income. At that point, Mateo was able to upgrade his equipment with the profit while still saving funds for future ventures.

Stay tuned to explore how this extra income opened doors to various opportunities, from setting ambitious savings goals to making his first investment decisions! We'll revisit Mateo's journey to witness how his unwavering determination propelled his gaming venture to even greater heights.

The Internet: Your Business Partner

As Sofia and Mateo discovered, the digital world is a vast playground, just waiting for you to explore. Whether you're into digital art, gaming, creating unique products, or any other exciting venture, turning your passion into cash is possible.

This is to say that technology is more than just a tool for consuming content. Your laptop, tablet, and phone become gateways to financial empowerment. The digital economy opens up endless possibilities for making money and providing services or products—anywhere, anytime, and for anyone.

Having a part-time job is one of many options for earning money. Starting an online business or a side hustle lets you bring your ideas to life. The best part? You get to be the boss and oversee every aspect of your venture! It's the process of transforming your ideas into a structured, money-making enterprise.

Exciting Side Hustles That Make Money

Now let's explore various paths to tickle your creative mind and ignite your entrepreneurial spirit. From the ordinary to the surprising, we have options that fit your skills and passions while providing you with the insights you need to kickstart your immediate path to success!

To set the stage for each of the concepts below, keep in mind that it is vital to stay ahead of the curve. Start your journey by following influencers and popular accounts in your chosen specialty on social media platforms like Instagram and TikTok. Dive into blogs and YouTube channels to find further insight into the latest trends and product reviews.

Another tip to remember is that building connections is essential. Join online groups that are related to your interests and engage in discussions so you can learn from fellow buyers and sellers. When you network with friends and peers who share your passions, they can provide you with a unique perspective on what's currently popular. Keep a watchful eye on trending hashtags across various social platforms to stay updated on the hottest trends in your chosen area of interest.

Online Retail: Embarking on a journey into retail can be a profitable endeavor for those who adore the thrill of the hunt and the joy of selling. If you're ready to transform your passion for shopping and socializing into a source of income, here's how to dive in.

First, begin by scouring various locations, from garage sales and flea markets to charity stores and sale racks at your favorite shops. Your mission is to unearth undervalued treasures waiting to be discovered. Whether it's vintage clothing, electronics, collectibles, or furniture, keep your eyes peeled for that diamond in the rough.

Next, use online platforms like eBay, Facebook Marketplace, and Depop to showcase and sell your finds. Create captivating listings with clear photos, detailed descriptions, and competitive prices. You want to attract potential buyers and close those sales!

Retail can yield a profit relatively quickly, depending on the items you find and the demand in your area. It's a low-risk way to make money, but substantial earnings are not guaranteed. So, while the journey can be exhilarating, remember that success comes with effort and savvy choices. Happy hunting!

Surveys, Reviews, and Product Testing: If you love diving into the latest gadgets, fashion trends, or mouthwatering snacks, turning your opinions into a source of income might be a fantastic idea. Many companies are eager to pay you to try out their products and share your honest thoughts through online reviews and surveys.

First, find reputable websites and platforms designed to connect product testers with companies. Steer clear of potential scams and look for well-known options like Toluna, Vindale Research, and Swagbucks. By registering on these platforms, you're taking your first step into this exciting world.

Once you're on board, you'll often be asked to fill out surveys or complete various tasks. These help companies match you with the right products. Be thorough and truthful in your responses; it increases your chances of receiving exciting products.

When you're selected to test a product, it's time for the real fun! Whether it's the latest tech gadget, trendy clothing, or a delicious snack, try it and take notes. Pay close attention to the product's features, quality, and pricing. Also, be sure to mention any suggested areas for improvement! Companies are usually eager for detailed feedback. Write thoughtful and honest reviews that highlight both the product's strengths and weaknesses.

Here's another cool part—this side hustle has room to expand in any direction you want to take it. Beyond writing a review for the testing company, consider posting them on your YouTube channel, social media profiles, or blog. Doing this can boost your online presence, opening doors to more opportunities and potential sponsorships.

It's essential to know that many product testing sites offer various forms of compensation. You might receive cash, gift cards, or even get to keep the products you've tested. Just be sure to read the fine print to stay informed.

With this opportunity, you can earn relatively quickly by sharing your opinions and testing products. It's a low-risk gig, but the reward might be moderate, depending on the surveys you qualify for and the number of products you are selected to test. When it comes down to it, if you're all about exploring the latest and greatest while making extra cash, this might be a perfect fit!

Content Creation: In the vast digital realm, opportunities to turn your creative endeavors into a source of income are boundless. You've likely heard stories of individuals making money through blogs or video-based platforms like YouTube, Instagram, and TikTok. If you prefer to remain anonymous, rest assured that you can create a faceless channel where your identity remains concealed, focusing solely on your written or filmed content.

The possibilities are endless, whether it's quotes, advice, or showcasing your photography skills. If you want to take your skills to the next level, consider incorporating AI-generated content for a unique twist. Whether you're passionate about a specific topic or have a beloved hobby, your journey into content creation can begin without emptying your wallet.

Content creation isn't limited to a single type or a particular niche. You can focus on multiple types of written or filmed material and explore many topics, whether cooking, beauty, tech, or anything that sparks your passion. The key is to create content that you're genuinely excited about.

For example, if you have a knack for words and dream of making money from the comfort of your room, starting a blog might be your ideal path. The beauty of it is that you don't need a significant upfront investment, but you do need dedication to create a loyal following who eagerly anticipates your next post. Start with selecting an effective and user-friendly platform for your blog like Blogger, Medium, Tumblr, Wix, or Weebly. While you don't have to be a professional writer, explore ways to improve your skills and begin looking into the basics of Search Engine Optimization to enhance your blog's discoverability.

Fine-tuning your writing abilities and mastering your video editing skills may take time, but it's a gratifying journey. To sustain your venture, keep producing and posting content, engage with your viewers, and consider investing in more advanced technology as you progress.

The beauty of content creation is that you can begin making money early in your journey by participating in what is known as affiliate marketing. As in Mateo's story, companies are often willing to pay you to display ads on your channel. Additionally, you can recommend products or services you genuinely believe in, potentially earning a commission for every sale through your referral links. Companies might even approach you to write about their products or services as your exposure grows.

Building a successful channel takes time, especially in the initial stages of attracting attention and followers. Be prepared for a journey that demands patience and a long-term perspective. The key is to stay persistent and continuously refine your content. The financial risk involved is minimal. You're primarily investing your time, creativity, and effort. However, the potential rewards are substantial, especially if your YouTube channel takes off by gaining at least 1000 subscribers and sponsors see you as a valuable partner. As you are working up to that point, offer your followers online tip jars and donation links to help you on your way!

Digital Artistry: If your heart beats to the rhythm of creativity, whether through drawing, painting, storytelling, musical expression, or design, the digital realm offers an open canvas for turning your passion into a flourishing venture. Let's look at a couple of practical ideas on how to set the stage for your earnings to take the spotlight.

Start by creating a digital portfolio to showcase your artistic prowess. Platforms like Etsy or Redbubble serve as your virtual art gallery. You don't need to be a professional artist, but a touch of skill can elevate your creations. From there, make sure to regularly generate and share new pieces to keep your audience engaged and eager for more.

If you have a combination of artistic passions that includes creative writing, graphic design, and educational instruction, another profitable avenue could be self-publishing low-content books on simple platforms like Amazon's Kindle Direct Publishing (KDP). The journey begins by choosing a niche, which can be anything from journals and organizers to coloring books or educational workbooks. From there, you can employ user-friendly design tools like Canva, Adobe Spark, Stencil, or word-processing software to craft your books, create catchy covers, and finalize them for publication. Whether you're designing pages, prompts, or templates for journals and planners or creating intricate designs for coloring books using apps like Procreate or Adobe Illustrator, the digital world is full of possibilities. In fact, since technology continues to improve and advance, keep an eye on AI's ability to create coloring book pages, book covers, and more digital imagery with the right prompts. It will only get more exciting from here!

With every type of digital artistry, it is important to continue honing your creative skills through workshops, online courses, and networking events. You might be surprised how often your local library or bookstore will pull together artists and writers to share fresh inspiration and up-to-date details about the latest trends within the art community.

One challenge with artistic ventures is how to get your physical product into the hands of a customer after they make a purchase. To help you navigate this, consider the pros and cons of each option, and then select the one that is best for you. For example, you can team up with print-on-demand services like Printful that transforms your art into tangible items like T-shirts, posters, and stickers, and Amazon's KDP produces low-content books for a special author's cost. This is a hassle-free approach; the best part is that you won't need substantial upfront investments.

Another option if you are seeking better control is to manage orders yourself, a hands-on approach that allows you to take charge of every step, from crafting the product to sending it out. Essentially, you're running your miniature art enterprise. The magic of this creative endeavor is that your creations remain available for people to purchase or utilize at any hour of any day. Your art becomes a 24/7 income generator, permitting you to earn money while you are busy working on your next dream!

Most of all, remember to use the full potential of social media platforms to publicize your products. Instagram, TikTok, and Pinterest are especially helpful at showcasing your work while still providing you with inspiration for future projects. Do what you can to build an artist platform and watch your success grow!

Artistic ventures carry minimal risk, especially since you won't need to invest much money upfront, just your time and some software or design tools. If you put in the effort and promote your art effectively, it has the great potential to bring in substantial earnings!

So, if you're a digital artist, the path from your imagination to your wallet is clear and accessible. It's a practical, budget-friendly way to monetize your talents and make money doing what you genuinely love.

These are just a couple of ways that you can use your passion, dedication, and the right skills to create a great side hustle! In reality, the list of possibilities is endless, so if your concept for a side hustle checks all the boxes, don't let anyone tell you that your idea is a bad one! Now, let's explore another example by learning how Dean turns his passion into a remarkable source of income while responsibly handling his finances.

Dean's Journey: From Creative Hobby to Thriving Business

Dean is a 19-year-old with a talent for digital art and poster design. His journey into transforming his passion into profit started when his part-time job at a local pizza shop reduced his hours. Looking for another way to make money, Dean opened an Etsy shop to showcase and sell his digital art and poster designs. He carefully curated his shop, displaying his portfolio and regularly updating it with samples of his work.

Dean didn't just wait for customers to find his shop; he got proactive. He promoted his shop and networked with everyone he knew—friends, family, potential customers, and fellow creatives. Plus, he used the internet to discover ways to improve his marketing skills so that he would succeed in his new venture. He regularly talked to other artists and joined discussions to get the lowdown on how to make his creative business thrive.

One ordinary day, Dean received his first order for a custom-designed poster! The client loved the finished product and left a glowing review, which boosted Dean's reputation. This success led to more custom requests, which also encouraged Dean to hone his graphic design skills for each new project.

As he took on more custom design requests, Dean enjoyed a steady income stream. Excited by the potential, he invested in better design software to enhance his capabilities and offer even more creative solutions to his clients. Each project taught him how to manage client expectations, meet deadlines, and understand the business side of running an Etsy shop.

Dean's side gig was flexible enough to complement his part-time job and other commitments. The freedom of running his Etsy shop allowed him to decide when to take on new projects.

Whether juggling classes or other responsibilities, a side hustle like this can seamlessly fit into your lifestyle. What begins as a creative outlet can quickly evolve into a dependable income source, showing that your passion can be a pathway to earning.

As he gains more visibility on Etsy, Dean may encounter the challenge of increased competition in the digital art and poster design market. Since he creates unique art and is working to continuously improve his skills, however, he will learn how to navigate the competition and provide exceptional service within a niche market to build an excellent reputation.

Another area that Dean will need to keep a close eye on is his finances. Initially, his earnings on Etsy will fluctuate depending on the demand, but by careful budgeting and planning, he will be able to keep his income balanced. At that point, Dean realizes that managing his Etsy shop is not only about creating stunning designs and satisfying his clients but also involves handling the financial side of the business.

Dean remembers the resources and advice that he has gained when making connections online. He knows that keeping detailed records of his earnings and expenses is crucial. By using Google Sheets, a free online spreadsheet tool, he sets up a simple system that provides a convenient and cost-effective way to track his income and manage his earnings. Dean records every payment that he receives for his digital art, custom poster designs, and other services and then keeps meticulous records of any purchases related to his shop. Some of the purchases that he made to improve his business include buying design software, investing in a better graphics tablet, and online ads to boost his social media presence.

With these steps in mind, Dean knows that being proactive about his money will make a big difference in his personal success and also make things a lot easier when tax season rolls around. We'll return to Dean's story later on and explore what he learned about credit when he decides to buy a new tablet, but in the meantime, let's think about taxes a bit more.

The IRS classifies successful business owners as self-employed once earnings from a side hustle or online business add up to $400. What does this mean for budding business owners like Dean or you? For starters, it means that all income from your online endeavors must be included when you file your tax return. But there's an exciting twist! Classifying your side hustle as an actual business means that you're also eligible for deductions, which can include new tools, digital equipment, or anything else that enhances your online work. If you carefully keep track of both purchases and expenses as Dean did, when tax season rolls around, you can subtract the cost of those upgrades from your taxable income and put a little money back in your wallet.

Reflection

> *"The only limit to our realization of tomorrow will be our doubts of today."*
>
> Franklin D. Roosevelt

You've just uncovered the exciting world of making money from an online venture or a side gig. The possibilities are truly boundless, and you can shape your path to financial success by following the tips in these pages. Think about your dreams, what you've learned, and your unique skills. As you focus on the road ahead, remember that each day is a chance to gain wisdom, develop, and craft the life you want.

Your financial adventure is only starting, and you can reach impressive heights by maintaining the right attitude! Start by asking yourself about the details that you will be required to take care of as you get into your desired side hustle, from how many initial costs are required to the amount of time that you will have to put into it all along. Also, think about the short-term and long-term factors, both the requirements and rewards for your desired gig, and if you are up for the commitment. While you are not promising to turn this side hustle into a full-time job for the rest of your life—though you certainly may if you have the passion and dedication to do so!—this is an important step forward in your early career.

Interactive Element: Dream Clouds Worksheet

Are you prepared to kindle your innovative spirit and awaken your creative spark? It's time to explore the dynamic world of side hustles on a personal level and learn how to transform your aspirations into tangible achievements.

In this activity, we'll use "Dream Clouds" to explore the depth of your creativity and generate ideas for potential side gigs. This worksheet is your canvas to sketch your ideal side hustle or other money-making adventure. Each cloud symbolizes a unique facet of the side hustle landscape, offering you diverse opportunities. Jot down your ideas in each cloud and let your imagination run wild. By the end of this activity, you'll have a list of potential business ventures. Get ready to dream big, ignite your creativity, and discover the endless possibilities for making money! Let's begin!

Cloud 1: Passions Ignited

Think about what makes your heart start racing with excitement. What are your hobbies and interests? What could you spend hours doing because you're passionate about it? Are there any activities that you enjoy so much that it causes you to lose track of time? Jot down your ideas.

Cloud 2: Real-Life Magic

Consider some everyday problems or inconveniences that you regularly encounter. If you could wave a magic wand and solve one issue or problem, what would it be? Write down some of these issues, why they are roadblocks for you, and what your magical solution would be to completely remove them from your path.

Cloud 3: Innovate Your Way

Imagine something that doesn't exist yet but would make your life or the life of a loved one better, easier, or more fun. What's your genius invention that would make you famous?

Cloud 4: Riding the Trends

Explore current trends and what's popular among you and your friends. Can you think of a way to recreate a cool concept, perhaps by giving it a new twist or making a better version of it? Record your trend-inspired concept.

Cloud 5: Your Hidden Superpower

Reflect on the positive things that people regularly say about you, especially the unique skills or talents that they have noticed in you. What is one thing that everyone says you're awesome at? Can you turn that superpower into a digital business? Capture your thoughts.

With those five clouds helping you organize some of your best ideas, can you see a pattern forming that will shape your passions and skills into the perfect area for a side hustle? As you begin to narrow down the possibilities, let's continue our exploration with another activity.

Interactive Element: Branding Brainstorm

Branding is vital to your entrepreneurial journey, shaping your business's identity, personality, and connection with customers. Let's follow these steps together to draft a memorable brand.

1. Name & Identity

- First, define your brand's personality, whether fun, professional, eco-conscious, or something else.
- Now, it's time to choose a catchy, relevant name that reflects your business according to the personality that you already defined.
- Tip: You can use the help of AI or ChatGPT to give you potential business names.

2. Logo Design

- Start by picking three colors that represent the personality of your side hustle.
- Create a simple, unique, recognizable logo using Canva or a similar design program by using those colors.
- You can also use free tools like Doodle Zone and Zarla to sketch and design your new logo.

3. Tagline

- Craft a catchy tagline that highlights what makes your side hustle unique.
- Once again, you are welcome to use the help of AI or ChatGPT to provide you with ideas, making sure to submit the right prompts that adequately explain the unique appealing aspects of your business so that you end up with a great list of potential tag lines.

4. Build a Strong Online Presence

- Create a free website and a good landing page with email marketing using a site like mailerlite.com that showcases

your products or services.
- Be active on the social media platforms that resonate the most with your target audience.

5. Use Storytelling

- Share your story, including why you have a passion for this business and what inspired you to start it.
- Describe your side hustle's personality as if it were a person so that it appeals more to your target audience.

Ready for the Next Step?

In exploring the practical ways that you can bring your dreams to life, you are probably realizing that this step of turning a simple hobby into an actual business is exciting and a little scary as well. It can especially be challenging to think about the financial details and all of the different ways that you need to manage the money that comes in and goes out.

As you follow up on your dream worksheet and branding brainstorm to take the next step, remember the examples of Sofia, Dean, and Mateo. These were young people who started just like you and were willing to take certain risks and think outside the box so they could reap the rewards of their dedication and perseverance!

Now, it's time to examine another essential aspect of managing your money—banking. Just as you've learned how to make money, you need to know how to keep it safe, make it work for you, and use it to prepare for your future. In the next chapter, we'll equip you with the knowledge and tools to master the banking world, helping you build a solid financial foundation. Get ready to uncover banking secrets and take your financial skills to the next level!

4

Banking Beyond the Basics

Three friends were at lunch at a local restaurant, bragging about how rich they were.

The one, a doctor, boasted that his income had doubled in the past five years because he had switched to a bigger hospital.

The second, a real estate agent, talked about how many houses she had sold in the past year during the housing boom and how her commission was the greatest out of all of her coworkers.

The third, a lawyer, showed a picture of a world-famous sports player and bragged how winning his case had earned him millions!

Meanwhile, an elderly farmer and his wife sat in the corner booth, overhearing the whole conversation. They smiled knowingly at each other, remembering that hospital salaries frequently change, housing booms tend to crash, and not every legal case is won.

These two hard-working people didn't have any fame or instant income to speak of, but they had obtained half of the town over the past several decades to support their growing enterprise, and founded the restaurant as well!

 "It's not how much money you make, but how much money you keep, how hard it works for you, and how many generations you keep it for."

Robert Kiyosaki

In the previous chapters, we've followed several different young people on their respective journeys in handling personal finances. Together, we've witnessed the power of a growth mindset, explored the diverse avenues of earning money, and seen how side hustles can morph into fulfilling careers.

Now, it's time to gear up for the next leg of this adventure—mastering modern banking. Are you curious about why banking is so crucial? The time to uncover secrets about the full potential of banking has arrived!

How Does Banking Work?

Let's catch up with Maya from our previous chapters. She's been working hard in her part-time job, and her efforts are paying off. Maya is in the same boat as many of you, trying to figure out how to manage her earnings effectively with the help of a bank account. Her goals are to master the art of banking, develop essential money management skills, and be yet another step closer to financial success.

First, Maya opens a savings account as a safe place to deposit her earnings, saving her from the hassle of carrying around a wad of cash that can easily be lost or stolen. Maya can access her funds easily by using the bank's app, allowing her to make deposits, track her balance, manage her expenses, pay bills, and set savings goals. With digital banking, she can check her account balance on her phone and even set up alerts to let her know when money comes in or goes out. Best of all, she can do this from the comfort of her home, school, or on the go!

"A simple fact that is hard to learn is that the time to save money is when you have some."

Joe Moore

The Features of a Savings Account

Let's take a step back for a moment. Before Maya opened her first account, she took the time to learn about her options and understand what kind of bank account would best meet her needs. She eventually chose a savings account to focus on tucking away a substantial portion of her hard-earned funds for the future.

When Maya first opened a savings account, the bank required her to put some money in right from the start. In her case, she only needed to deposit $25, which was perfect for her budget after having saved up cash from her babysitting gigs.

Maya also learned that some savings accounts have a rule that a certain amount of money must remain in the bank, an amount known as a minimum balance. If she withdrew that amount, the bank would penalize her with a fee. Maya's account required a minimum balance of $25, which worked out perfectly because that was the exact amount that she was depositing.

Speaking of fees, Maya was careful to research those sneaky bank charges and what she needed to do to avoid them. Her goal was to keep her money safe and growing, so she made sure that her savings account was "free," which meant that the bank did not charge her any monthly or yearly fees.

Next, Maya studied up on interest rates. She learned that putting money in some accounts would reward her with a small percentage in return, known as interest. She understood that having an account with a higher interest rate meant that her savings would grow even more and help her reach her financial goals faster! So, she picked an account with a higher interest rate that would keep her on track to greater savings.

Maya was all about convenience and needed a bank account that would match her fast-paced life. The last thing she searched for was to make doubly sure that her bank of choice came with a mobile app that was super easy to navigate. She was happy to find out that the app let her check her balance whenever she wanted and wherever she was, assuring her that her money was growing. It was like having a personal financial assistant right at her fingertips, just a tap away!

The final topic that Maya researched was about her spending options. Her mindset was on savings, but she was happy to learn that most savings accounts come with a monthly allowance of six transactions, essentially because they are not intended for regular spending. She knew that her savings account would help her with money growth, and that if she ever needed more spending options, she would consider a checking account for her day-to-day expenses.

The Basics of a Checking Account

How could Maya open a bank account while she was still under the age of 18? In the United States, typically, minors can't open their own checking or savings account unless they're legally emancipated. Many financial institutions, however, allow young people under 18 to open a joint account with a parent or guardian. This means that a responsible adult also has their name on the account so that they can provide oversight and guidance.

In Maya's case, her mom agreed to open a joint savings account so that they could make deposits and withdrawals together. In their research prior to going to the bank, Maya and her mom discovered that the following banks offer a number of different account options for young people:

- Wells Fargo: Teen Checking
- Bank of America: Student Banking
- Chase: First Banking
- Capital One: Kids Savings Account
- PNC Bank: PNC 'S' is for Savings
- TD Bank: TD Simple Savings

Keep in mind that account types, interest rates, reward programs, and specific requirements change over time. For the latest details, check out current information online! Links to these account options are provided in the resources page.

Dreaming Big: Mateo's Path to Financial Success

Let's check in with Mateo, too, our gaming wizard. He transformed his passion for gaming into a YouTube channel. This got real once his videos started racking up views and he began making money from ads. Now, Mateo faces a big question: "How should I handle my hard-earned cash?"

He has always tried to be smart with his money, so he opened a savings account when first making income and has been saving a portion for an upcoming ski trip. Now, he decides that it is time to open a checking account. Mateo understands that having a savings relationship already established at his bank means that he has access to additional benefits!

Like Maya, Mateo doesn't have a lot of extra cash to deposit. He chooses to open a free checking account that only requires $25 up front. As a busy gamer, video producer, and YouTube channel manager, Mateo also needs an account that makes online deposits and transfers a breeze. That's where the real magic of mobile banking comes into play. With the power of mobile apps and features, Mateo can easily request a direct deposit to his bank from YouTube to his smartphone. No more rushing to the bank or ATM! He can do everything from the comfort of his gaming chair. It's like having a bank teller in his pocket!

Also, whenever Mateo needs cash for gaming tournaments or late-night snack runs, he has many different possibilities to choose from. What could make his situation better? For cash, there are many different ATMs part of his bank's network, meaning that he can use them without facing any extra fees. Mateo can also make payments right from his phone at any number of major retailers.

Even better, many checking accounts today offer a range of features and rewards to sweeten the deal. For instance, Wells Fargo offers a Teen Checking Account that provides access through a debit card, mobile app, and online banking. The mobile app offers budgeting tools, and the debit card allows for cashback rewards. Mateo chooses Discover Bank's Cashback Debit Account, which allows him to earn cashback rewards every time he makes a purchase.

So, whether you're into gaming, shopping, or just want to make your money work a little harder, there's likely a checking account out there that suits your goals. It's all about finding the one that matches your lifestyle and priorities to make the most of your banking experience. We'll catch up with Mateo later to see how his current money choices result in more innovative financial moves later on!

 "It is our choices that show what we truly are, far more than our abilities."

J.K. Rowling

Interactive Element: Savings vs. Checking Showdown

Let's take a deeper look into the similarities and differences between checking and savings accounts, using an activity to measure them up against each other.

Instructions:

1. Create a Venn Diagram: Draw two overlapping circles and write titles above them with one being "Checking Account" and the other being "Savings Account."

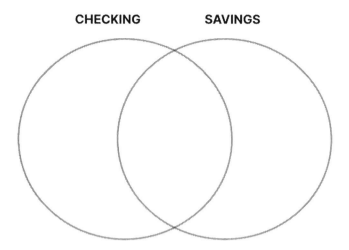

2. List the Benefits: Think about what each type of account offers and write it inside their respective circles. What makes checking accounts rock? What makes savings accounts shine?

✢ Checking Account Advantages:

- Access to your money 24/7
- Personal debit card
- Conveniently withdraw money from an ATM

✢ Savings Account Advantages:

- Opportunity to earn interest
- Helps you save for the future
- Safe place to keep your money

3. List the Disadvantages: Below each circle, jot down any not-so-cool stuff about these accounts including fees and restrictions.

— Checking Account Disadvantages:

- You usually don't earn interest with this type of account

- Possible monthly fees
- Best for money moving in and out, not for saving

— Savings Account Disadvantages:

- Limited transactions per month
- Possible minimum deposit required

4. Find the Common Ground: For the area where the circles overlap, look for things that checking and savings accounts both share.

Things in Common:

- Extra-safe money in an insured bank!
- Tech-friendly options for both online and phone banking options
- Great for planning your finances

5. Reflect and Share: Once your Venn diagram is complete, take a moment to think about what you've learned and how to present it to a friend or your family. You'll be surprised at how much you can share with others!

Strategy Power Up: Bank on Technology

If you're not ready to open a bank account, there is no need to worry! There are a lot of money management apps that don't require you to have a traditional bank account. They're designed to be user-friendly, making it a breeze for anyone who's new to money management. These apps allow you to easily budget, save, and even send money to friends. They prioritize your security, helping you keep your personal and financial details safe. Plus, some of these apps come with educational tools to help you master the art of money management. If you're looking for a modern, hassle-free way to handle your finances, these apps are worth exploring!

Prepaid Debit Card Apps: Many prepaid debit cards come with mobile apps that allow you to manage your funds without having a traditional bank account. These apps provide features like direct deposit, bill payment, and budgeting tools. Let's take a look at several popular options.

PayPal: While not a traditional bank, PayPal offers a range of financial services, including a mobile app for managing your balance, direct deposit, making payments, and even linking to a debit card.

Cash App: Created by Square, Cash App allows you to send and receive money, invest in stocks, and manage your cash balance.

Venmo: Owned by PayPal, Venmo is primarily used for sending and receiving money between friends but also allows you to keep a balance within the app without the need for a bank account.

Simple: This is an online-only bank that provides a money management app for users to budget, save, and track their spending. While it is a bank, it's not a traditional one, and you can use its features without a bank account.

These apps come in handy for your everyday financial needs. To find the option that's just right for you, make sure to check out the unique features that each one offers and any associated fees. It's all about finding the perfect fit for your management style!

Money Management Checklist

Now for your ultimate money management checklist! These essential steps make up a personal roadmap to help you make smart money moves and reach financial empowerment.

1. Know Your Money Goals. First, decide what you want to save and spend money on. Include both short-term and long-term goals to help you keep the right perspective.

2. Pick a Financial Institution. Next, it's time to look for a bank or credit union that welcomes young adults. In your research, make sure to find one with low fees and no strict rules.

Let's pause a moment to further explain credit unions, which are similar to banks but are a special kind of financial institution that requires you to become a member before holding accounts with them. For instance, if your parents or employer are members, then you can be invited to a membership through them. Credit unions are more competitive than banks, often have minimum deposit requirements, include lower fees, and have better interest rates.

3. Open Your Account(s). It's time to make it happen! Visit the financial institution of your choice in person or complete the necessary paperwork online. If you're under 18 years old, you'll need a parent or guardian as a joint account holder to help you complete this step.

4. Master the Mobile App. As a final step, download the bank's app and familiarize yourself with the following features:

- Check your balance
- Review your recent purchases
- Send money

- Set up reminders to make a payment or check your balance
- Pay a bills
- Deposit checks on your phone

You have successfully opened your first bank account. Congratulations!

Reality Check: A Lesson in Hidden Fees

Remember 19-year-old Dean from our last chapter? He's a super saver with a unique talent for graphic design. The more creativity he pours into his designs, the more he realizes he can turn his passion into a side hustle. His artistic creations are not only a hit with friends and family but also among others who find his online portfolio.

As demand for his designs grows, Dean decides to open a bank account to manage his earnings. He wants a secure place to stash his hard-earned cash with the convenience of easy access. Opening a checking account is a no-brainer; he needs it to receive regular payments from his clients.

However, in his excitement to start his banking journey, Dean misses something crucial—understanding the fine print about limitations and restrictions. Since he already signed the necessary paperwork, these are nitty-gritty details that he unknowingly agreed to.

Weeks pass, and Dean continues to rake in payments for his graphic design work. Everything seems to be smooth sailing until he notices something strange while checking his account balance online. It is suddenly showing charges that he never spent with his debit card! Dean cannot fathom why this is happening! He begins to feel a bit confused, and a hint of worry sets in. Immediately, he calls the bank, hoping for answers.

The bank representative reviews Dean's account and informs him that he has been charged with monthly maintenance fees! Dean's heart sinks. He did not know about these sneaky fees when opening the account! Fortunately, the bank rep is understanding, reverses the fees, and takes the time to share more details about hidden costs in banking. These pesky charges can hit at different times—for monthly maintenance, overdrafts, or even using ATMs from other banks.

It is a lightbulb moment for Dean. Like any business, banks are out to make a profit! So, sometimes they use these fees to achieve their financial goals. This experience teaches him the value of financial knowledge and the necessity of staying vigilant about hidden charges. With this newfound awareness about financial details, Dean gets his account straightened out and ends the call with gratitude for the lessons learned.

By understanding the business side of banking, you can also make informed choices about where to stash your money and how to avoid unnecessary charges. Remember, it's all part of your money journey, and each lesson learned gets you one step closer to financial empowerment.

Sofia's Digital Piggy Bank

Sofia first starts selling her jewelry at local craft fairs and has a humble online presence. Her unique jewelry pieces quickly catch the eye of customers, and her business starts to flourish. However, the traditional cash transactions are becoming cumbersome and even a bit risky.

A fellow artist suggests that Sofia think about using a digital wallet like Cash App or Venmo as potential solutions. As she starts her research, Sofia learns that these apps allow her to accept payments with ease. All her customers need to do is scan a QR code, and the transactions are complete in just a few seconds! No more fumbling for exact change, and no more worrying about keeping cash safe! Sofia's digital wallet also keeps track of every sale for her, making it a breeze to manage her earnings and expenses on her Google Spreadsheet.

Whether you're running an online business, starting a side hustle, or simply looking to streamline your everyday transactions, digital wallets are like your personal financial assistant, making life more convenient, secure, and fun. With just a smartphone in hand, you can handle payments, track your expenses, and even set savings goals. So, when you're ready to take your financial management to the next level, digital wallets are a fantastic option to explore.

Interactive Element: Mastering Money Management

Now let's take a look at an activity that will help us put financial tracking into practice. First, let's summarize Sofia's journey as a small business.

When Sofia first started her online store, she saved up $100.00 as her starting capital. Her jewelry began to sell, and the orders started rolling in. Her first customer bought a bracelet for $10.00. This was her very first sale, and she excitedly recorded it as a deposit.

As word of mouth spread about Sofia's Creations, more orders came in. A friend purchased two bracelets for $20.00, and another customer ordered a customized necklace for $30.00. Sofia was thrilled by the demand and recorded these sales as deposits as well.

At that point, Sofia needed to buy more supplies to keep up with the growing demand. She spent $15.00 on quality gemstones and wires. She marked this expense as a withdrawal.

Sofia also wanted to attract more customers to her Instagram store, so she ran an ad campaign that cost her a total of $10.00. Although it was an expense, she saw it as an investment in her business's growth.

Then there was Sofia's goal that she had since she first opened her business: purchasing a new set of tools to expand her jewelry line. She decided to transfer $20.00 from her checking account to her savings account, taking a tangible step to save for the future of her business.

Sofia learned that her finances required attention and care as an important part of her jewelry business. Ultimately, her story shows the importance of knowing the difference between deposits and withdrawals. By being able to practice these activities, it causes Sofia to realize that being cautious and managing her money wisely is essential for her long-term goals.

It's time for your Money Management Challenge! In the table below, you'll find a blank bank account ledger. Go back through Sofia's story once more, following her journey and filling in the blanks to discover current checking account balance. We'll get you started on the first transaction!

Sofia's Bank Account

Date	Transaction Details	Deposit	Withdrawal	Balance
October 19	Initial Deposit	$100.00		$100.00

Instructions for Each Column:

1. Date: Feel free to make these up as you go along
2. Transaction Details: Record each reason Sofia either earned or spent money
3. Deposit: Mark down the amount each time Sofia received money and put it into her checking account. Add this value to her total balance.
4. Withdrawal: Record the amount each time Sofia spent money on her business. Subtract this value from the total balance.
5. Balance: Update this column every time a transaction takes place to keep track of Sofia's available funds.

Bonus Questions:

1. What is the total income that Sofia's business has brought in since she started?
2. Using the same method, how much money has Sofia spent on her business?

Even in an age of handy money apps, understanding the fundamentals of managing money flow for your own bank account is crucial. This hands-on activity helps you practice basic accounting principles, make informed decisions, monitor your money effectively, and develop a deeper sense of financial empowerment. It's like learning the rules of the game before you step out and start playing—it gives you a solid foundation for lifelong financial success!

It All Goes Back to Mindset!

In this past chapter, we've walked through the banking world and created a solid base for responsibly tracking your income and expenditures. The journey highlighted the reasons for owning a bank account for smart spending and saving and mentioned some of the features that the most popular types of bank accounts offer. We've also learned to be aware of hidden fees and requirements that banks might throw your way.

In increasing your knowledge about banking, it is less about the mere mechanics of accounts and all about embracing the right mindset required to navigate the financial landscape successfully. Just take a moment to think back over the themes that we have already learned and how they all come together—by cultivating a positive growth mindset, taking practical steps to acquire a job for consistent income, and exploring ways to turn your passion into a profit for even greater financial independence, you are setting yourself up for financial security and wealth! Now, with this added insight about the ins and out of banking, you have yet another powerful tool in your money kit to help you achieve your long-term financial goals.

So, where do we go from here? It's time to consider developing financial wisdom and further empowering your mindset to transform your dreams into achievable realities. In other words, opening a bank account is just the first step to understanding spending and saving money. It's important to have control of your money for a very important benefit—bringing you closer to security, freedom, and wealth! Unlocking your financial potential means learning how to invest your money, save it wisely, make smart spending decisions, and more. Your wealth is more than just growing numbers on a balance sheet; it's the sum of your aspirations and your ability to turn your dreams into reality!

Bridging the Financial Education Gap

"An investment in knowledge pays the best interest."

Benjamin Franklin

It's unfortunate that financial education isn't something you can get in school, not least because it's impossible to chase it on your own and trust that you're getting real information... and not just a lot of cleverly disguised *mis*information.

The truth is that a lot of young people are looking for an accessible and trustworthy financial education just as you are – because they know that understanding all things money is important, especially if they're to reach that goal that we all want: financial freedom. You're discovering everything you need to know to pave the way for reaching that goal, and that means a life in which you can do the things you truly want to do instead of a life where you're stuck behind a desk day in and day out.

We want as many young people as possible to have that opportunity, and I'm sure you agree that since this isn't something you're taught in school, we need to take a different approach. So at this stage in our journey together, I'd like to ask for your help in reaching more teenagers and young adults.

The good news is, that's dead easy, and it won't take more than a few minutes. All I'd like to ask you to do is leave a short review.

By leaving a review of this book on Amazon, you'll show other young people exactly where they can find the complete yet accessible financial education they're looking for.

Your review will act as a signpost, pointing new readers in the direction of the advice they're already looking for – and it will inspire them to take action now to pave the way for the future they truly want to have.

Thank you so much for your help. We couldn't do this without you.

Scan the QR code below for a quick review!

5

The Saving and Spending Blueprint

Do you know what method is the single best way to manage your money, but one that is often overlooked? Here's a hint: It involves putting funds in a safe place and keeping them there. Yes, you guessed it right – that method is saving!

Why is saving such a hard thing to do? It often seems that as soon as income flows in, everyone is competing to take a piece of the pie from you. Not only that but saving often gets moved to the back burner because it is so easy to think about purchasing things that you may either need or want as soon as you have the funds to cover it.

This chapter provides you with a reality check – the way that you and saving money work together sets you up for your financial future. In other words, learning how to save is such a crucial part of money management that without it, you will be pointing your steps toward certain financial hardship. When you actively prioritize saving, however, you set yourself up for a safe, happy, and healthy future!

Are you ready to set sail into the world of money management? Picture yourself as the captain of your own boat, steering your course down the river of money. As you make important decisions, you call the shots that can either lead you to the clear, cool, refreshing lake of prosperity and freedom or land you in the murky swamp of poverty and struggle!

To help you navigate the waters, let's break down the details about saving and spending along with everything that goes into it – earning an allowance, selling your own product or service, obtaining financial freedom, and more. By the end of this chapter, you will be able to understand, control, and use your cash flow to your greatest advantage!

 "It's not your salary that makes you rich; it's your spending habits."

Charles A. Jaffe

Mastering Cash Flow

Making smart financial decisions isn't just about knowing how everything happens. It goes back to having a growth mindset and using your knowledge of cash management to benefit your long-term goals. Having said that, let's start with the basics of how money comes in and out and then dive in deeper for a greater understanding of how to make it work for you.

Money regularly flows in and out of your bank account. When money flows in – usually because you received your allowance, a well-earned paycheck, special birthday presents, or similar reasons – then your bank balance goes up. On the other hand, your bank account takes a hit every time you make a purchase, whether it's getting a new outfit, buying midnight snacks, paying bills and other expenses, or locking in savings for a big dream.

Let's check in with Sofia to see how she is balancing the basics of cash flow. She recently attended her first art festival and sold 30 pieces of jewelry, which was a significant boost to both her confidence and her income! At the same time, however, her business involves regular expenses, which requires her to calculate her actual net income. Sofia determines that her income outweighs her outgoing cash, but that is not always true for everyone. By mirroring her actions with the specifics of your own situation, you will be able to evaluate your current financial health. Take a look at the following steps:

1. Start with the total amount brought in: Sofia sold 25 bracelets at $7 each.

Total Revenue = 25 bracelets x $7 per bracelet = $175

2. Next, subtract the total expenses: Sofia spent $50 on materials.

Total Expenses = $50

3. To find the net cash flow, subtract the total expenses from the total revenue.

Net Cash Flow =$175
- $50
$125

Sofia's net cash flow after the fair was $125, which means she has more money coming in than she has going out. Sofia is on track for financial success! In this exercise, she discovers the secret to growing her bank account: Making sure the money she has coming in outweighs the money that is going out!

Here's another tip: If you find yourself spending more than you're earning, it's time to rethink your financial strategies. When you make savvy decisions with your cash, you will watch that balance shoot up. The next time you check your bank balance, tuck money away for future adventures, or click "buy" online, tell yourself, "My money is a powerful tool, and with the right choices, I'm steering my own course toward financial success!"

Interactive Element: Cash Flow Showdown

Let's practice the concept with Net Cash Flow some more with Mateo's story as our backdrop. First, let's recap the definitions:

Money In: Funds that you're earning or receiving.

Money Out: Money that you're spending.

Net Cash Flow: Subtract the Money Out from Money In.

>   Is it positive? You've made a profit!
>   Is it negative? You've spent more than you earned!

Mateo, who transformed his passion for gaming into a thriving YouTube channel, regularly shares his gameplay videos and keeps his audience entertained with witty commentary. As his subscribers and fan base grow, he introduces a donation button on his channel. This month, between his ad campaign income and the generous support from his viewers, his money adds up to a total of $150.

Now, let's talk about his expenses. Mateo understands the importance of a stable and high-speed internet connection to maintain top-notch streaming quality and ensure smooth uploads. To keep things running seamlessly, he incurs a monthly expense of $50 for his internet service. Additionally, he recently bought the latest video game for his upcoming series on the channel, setting him back $60 – an investment to keep his gaming venture going strong!

Now, let's help Mateo calculate his net cash flow!

1. Calculate the total money received this month (Money In).
2. Calculate the money spent on internet charges and the new game (Money Out).
3. Subtract the total money spent (Money Out) from the money received (Money In).

Net Cash Flow (Money In - Money Out): _____

Can you determine if Mateo had a positive cash flow this month, indicating that he made a profit from his YouTube Gaming channel? OR Was his cash flow negative?

"Money is only a tool. It will take you wherever you wish, but it will not replace you as the driver."

Ayn Rand

Future-Focused Budgeting

Now it's time to talk about a smart financial move that sounds boring but can be exciting – creating a budget! You can jot it down in a notebook, create a carefully formatted document on your computer, or use whatever method suits your style.

First things first, list all of the cash that you expect to regularly come in, including your allowance and any earnings. Then, think about any expenses that you may face, whether it is a monthly phone bill, monetary gifts, or transfers into a special savings account for the future. This forms the foundation for your budget.

Next up, you want to keep a close eye on where your money goes. Every time you swipe that card or pull cash out of your wallet, it's time to add it to your budget. Yes, this even includes those fun shopping trips with friends!

Now comes the important part for fine-tuning your budget – comparing what you're actually raking in to what you're dishing out. Ideally, your income should be more than your expenses. If it's not, don't stress! We'll help you fine-tune your money game.

Here's another tip: There are awesome money management apps like "PocketGuard" and "Clarity Money" to help you track your spending and keep track of your money goals. These are like financial wizards in your pocket, showing you your saving wins and where you might be overdoing it in the spending category.

Finally, it's time to go back and fine-tune your budget so it fits your vibe! It doesn't have to be old, stodgy, and boring like an accountant's spreadsheet. It can be fun and match your personality! Get practical with your finances in a way that suits your unique saving and spending style. When it comes down to it, creating a budget helps you make smart choices while still enjoying the things you love. Let's give budget-making a try with a fun and effective activity below!

Interactive Element: Your Budget, Your Way

Step 1: Find Your Starting Point

Before diving into budgeting, let's figure out where your money is coming from and where it's going. Take a moment to list your income sources. If you have a part-time job, allowances, or any other source of income, jot it down.

Step 2: Track Your Spending

Now, let's see where your money is going. For one week, keep a record of every penny you spend. This will give you a clear picture of your spending habits.

Step 3: Set Your Financial Goals

What do you want to achieve with your money? Think about your short-term and long-term goals. Do you want to save for a trip, a new gadget, or higher education? Is it important to have an emergency fund? Write these things down.

A Note about Emergency Funds: It's important to consider setting aside money that goes into your savings account in case of an emergency. You can't predict needing to replace a flat tire, losing your part-time job, or suddenly being without a roommate after yours suddenly moved out and left you with the full rent. Your Emergency Fund can come in handy when faced with unexpected expenses!

Step 4: Categorize Your Expenses

Take a look at your spending records and categorize your expenses. Common categories include:

- Essentials (food, transportation, housing)
- Entertainment (movies, gaming, eating out)

- Savings (investing, preparing for future goals)
- Unexpected (emergencies, unplanned expenses)

Step 5: Set Spending Limits

Based on your goals and spending habits, set limits for each spending category. Be realistic and ensure there's some room for fun!

Step 6: Stick to Your Budget

The most important step is to stick to your budget. Keep track of your expenses regularly and adjust where needed.

Step 7: Review and Reflect

At the end of each month, review how well you stuck to your budget. Did you achieve your goals? If yes, great! If not, don't stress – just adapt and keep going. The more you practice each month, the better you will get at this crucial skill!

Tips for Budgeting Success:

- Balance is Key: Make sure your budget includes both saving and spending for things you enjoy. It's about finding a balance.
- Emergency Fund: Always set aside some money for emergencies, even if it's just a small amount.
- Apps Are Your Friends: Consider using budgeting apps like the ones mentioned previously. Or check out "Mint" or "You Need a Budget" to help you keep track of your spending effortlessly.
- Stay Flexible: Life happens, and sometimes you need to adjust your budget. That's okay!
- Reward Yourself: Don't forget to celebrate your achievements when you reach your financial goals.

Budgeting is a smart move that can help you enjoy life while ensuring your financial future is solid. Make it your own and watch your money work for you.

 "You must gain control over your money or the lack of it will forever control you."

Dave Ramsey

Save with Purpose

Now it is time to talk more about the importance of saving. In today's fast-paced world, money can disappear as quickly as it comes in. What if every dollar you earned had a specific purpose? The heart of intentional saving is understanding why you're doing it. Do you dream of traveling, furthering your education, starting a business, or exploring a new passion? Your savings can transform those dreams into reality!

Even greater than those temporary goals are the ones that help you set up a plan for financial independence and security. As you save with purpose, you are not stashing money randomly – it's about laying the groundwork for investments, acquiring assets, and exploring various ways to grow your wealth so that your money continues to work for you far into your future.

 Money expands my life's opportunities and experiences. I am creating an abundant future for myself and my family!

Set Savings Goals

One of the most exciting aspects of intentional saving is having specific goals to strive towards. Start by defining your savings goals. As with any goal, the best way to set them up for success is to ensure they are SMART: specific, measurable, achievable, relevant, and time-bound. This is to say that your savings plan is possible to accomplish because it is grounded within a realistic timeframe that works for you. Whatever the details may be, be clear about the direction you are headed toward and the purpose of each goal.

Within your SMART goals, there are two timeframes to keep in mind. Short-term goals are like the fun pit stops on your financial journey that take place every few months. For instance, you might treat yourself to a memorable day with friends, buy concert tickets to see your favorite band, or invest in new equipment for your online startup.

Long-term financial goals are the real game-changers! These are dreams that might take years or even decades to accomplish, but they're worth every bit of planning and saving. Picture investing money for the future that can go into any number of things—buying your first car, traveling to exciting destinations, preparing for early retirement, or expanding your small business into a larger venture that makes a real mark on the world!

As you set your goals, consider using an app like "Qapital," which helps you track your savings for future success. You can break down larger objectives into manageable chunks and watch your progress. This saving methodology is a powerful motivator and a practical way to ensure your financial dreams become a reality, being your guiding stars that help bring your dreams that much closer.

In this next activity, let's practice putting your dreams on paper and creating a visual map that keeps you inspired and on track. As you get ready to map out your financial journey, recognize that your goals are closer than you think!

Interactive Activity: Mapping Your Financial Dreams

It's time to take your financial game to the next level! With your budget in hand and your dreams in mind, let's dive into creating a money map by following along with Lydia, a 17-year-old athlete who is looking forward to an exciting summer.

1. Define Your Short-Term Goals:

When Lydia thinks about what she wants to achieve in the next few months, she comes up with a list of questions to consider:

- What are my upcoming priorities?
- Are there any upcoming expenses I need to plan for?
- What would make my current situation better?
- What small things or experiences do I want to treat myself to?
- What's an achievement that would make me super proud?
- What's at the top of my to-do list right now?

As a head cheerleader, one of Lydia's top goals is to find a way to throw an appreciation party for her squad by the end of the school year. She also wants to attend several exciting summer sports camps in preparation for the fall soccer season. Then there is her dream to give her little sister an amazing 12th birthday party, and while her mom would cover the majority of the expenses, she has some cool ideas that she wants to chip in for. All of these things fall under Lydia's short-term goals!

2. Imagine Your Long-Term Dreams:

From there, Lydia begins to dream big about her financial future. Here are some questions that she uses to get her wheels turning:

- Where do I picture myself in a few years?
- What are my loftiest dreams and ambitions?
- What cool stuff do I want to own or experience in the future?
- What significant accomplishments do I want to achieve down the road?

As an athlete who loves all sports, Lydia can see herself being a varsity level coach in the future. To prepare for that, she wants to absorb all of the sports education available to her, starting with her own college experience and moving on to specialized certifications that will bring her recognition in the sports world! To help her financially prepare, Lydia knows that she will need to be disciplined to save for a college education, even with the sports scholarships that she is eligible to apply for.

3. Prioritize Your Goals:

Now, it's time for Lydia to list both her short-term and long-term goals. At first, she thought this was difficult to do based on how many dreams she had and how each one depended upon the next. It became easier as she focused on identifying her top three goals and putting a monetary figure on each one.

Lydia took several actionable steps by thinking about these guiding questions:

- What's the exact cost of this goal?
- How much money will I need to reach each one?
- What's my deadline for achieving each goal?

- Will I set aside money weekly or monthly to make it happen?
- Are there any opportunities that can help me reach my goals faster?

By mapping out your financial dreams like Lydia has, you're not just planning for your future – you're taking control of it! You're crafting a detailed blueprint for your financial future that is not just about numbers. Your journey is about to become that much more meaningful because you are owning it by directing each of your experiences and achievements!

Understanding Your Purchases

In emphasizing the importance of saving, we also want to take a careful look at the decision-making process when it comes to spending money. Having a good budget is not just about exercising your newfound knowledge of financial matters; it's making sure that your spending and savings are in sync with what you value and aspire to achieve.

This is to say that your spending habits should always mirror your identity, priorities, and life goals. Since your daily choices can either steer you toward success or land you in ruin, it is critical to be knowledgeable and disciplined in the spending department.

To begin this discussion, let's differentiate between wants and needs. We're often bombarded with advertisements, endorsements, and recommendations that push us to believe that we actually "need" whatever a particular company is selling. This hype can blur the distinction between what we genuinely need and what we desire for the time being. In moments like these, it is critical to take a step back for the sake of clarity and consider what is truly necessary.

Is It Worth It?

Ultimately, everything you buy should bring joy and fulfillment to your life. So, be honest with yourself prior to every purchase and assess whether you're using your newly obtained goods to their full potential for your life. Ask yourself: "Is____worth it?"

This question provides a reality check to guide you toward more satisfying and enjoyable spending decisions that resonate with who you are and where you want to go in life.

Another way to practice this is to consider a "cooling-off" period before a purchase. This simple practice involves stepping back and giving yourself time to think through the value of the item, determining whether you genuinely need the item or merely want it on a passing whim.

Going back to Mateo for a moment, he learned early on in his gaming career about the intense pressure to constantly buy new upgrades. From the very first time he made his first purchase, he began receiving regular emails, texts, and pop-up notifications telling him that his software needed to be upgraded or that he was next in line for a big promotional offer.

At first, Mateo began to feel frustrated, thinking that there was no way he could afford all of the latest updates to remain a top-notch gamer. He even bought one of the special promo offers for "the low price of $39.99," but was disappointed to discover that it only contained several features and extra skins that he would never use.

Fortunately, he was on a couple great forums and followed several expert-level gamers who advised him of the most important upgrades and told him to ignore the rest as deceptive advertising! Mateo learned an important lesson to always do his research before making any future purchases, giving himself that valuable space to think and consider his needs and wants.

As you consider purchases, ask yourself several more questions – Do I need this item for my daily needs, whether food, shelter, or utilities? Or, is it an unnecessary expense? If this is a want, will it add enjoyment to my life, or will it negatively impact my budget so that I regret it later? These are realistic questions to carefully consider and will give us more insight into the big picture of our lives!

The Art of Smart Spending

Let's take a look at Dean's journey to see how he handles the challenge of balancing his wants and needs when crafting his budget!

When we first met him in Chapter 1, Dean was working through letting go of a limiting mindset that was passed down from his family as they regularly dealt with financial struggles. He often grew up hearing, "Money doesn't grow on trees" or "We can't afford that," making it easy for Dean to believe that money was scarce. Saving money felt like a foreign concept. His journey was further complicated by social media, where friends flaunted expensive Christmas presents and extravagant vacations that he had never experienced before.

As he took a step back from his own situation, Dean began to question his impulsive spending habits that often followed each paycheck from his part-time job. It was frustrating to change his habits, but Dean knew that true wealth went beyond owning high-end sneakers or the latest smartphone. He recognized that real empowerment meant making choices that aligned with his authentic self, and he was ready to address his lack of money management skills head-on.

Dean began by creating a document on his computer that allowed him to meticulously track his earnings and expenses. This was an eye-opener! He realized that his frequent visits to the local coffee shop and online shopping sprees were eating into his earnings.

In response to his findings, Dean made a goal to save 20% of each paycheck in his savings account. After a year, his commitment to discipline and determination was finally rewarded! He had saved enough to purchase the camera of his dreams, igniting his passion to learn and enact even more financial knowledge!

The story didn't end there. Dean was fueled by his newfound information, and he embarked on a thrilling journey of entrepreneurship. His photography skills led to a brilliant idea – conveniently offering personalized pet portrait services at the client's home. It was a win-win; he pursued his passion while generating extra income.

Interactive Element: Spending Self-Check Worksheet

Dean learned that making choices that reflect your true self is the key to financial empowerment. The Spending Self-Check Worksheet will help you reflect on your recent purchases, just like Dean did. By aligning your spending with your values and interests, you can make sure your money is going toward things that truly matter to you!

Part 1

- Write down the last three items you bought that could be classified as non-essential.
- Think about the real value of each purchase. Were they wants or needs?

- Reflect on whether you would still desire these items if you hadn't come across them on social media.
- Consider how these purchases align with your interests, values, or passions.
- Describe the feelings these purchases generated.
- Evaluate if you use or enjoy these items as much as you initially expected.

Part 2

- List 3-5 core values that are important to you (e.g., sustainability, education, family time, health, creativity).
- Next to each value, write down a purchase or expenditure to match it.
- Reflect: Go back to your list of purchases from Part 1.
- Assess how well these items match up with your values list.
- Identify any discrepancies between your purchases and your core values.
- Consider what adjustments you might make in your future spending decisions to better align with your values!

This valuable activity offers you a clear opportunity to take control of your spending habits and make more meaningful choices. By doing so, you gain insight into what truly matters, differentiate between what you want and what you need, and determine how well your spending aligns with your personal values and interests. Ultimately, this activity empowers you to make wiser spending decisions and leads to stronger connections with the things that genuinely resonate with you.

Another great lesson that this teaches is that your money mindset is not set in stone! Even as Dean was able to recognize his financial mistakes based on his inherited beliefs and overcome those errors, your mindset can also change as you learn more about managing your finances and how to achieve your financial goals. By better understanding your money blueprint and making informed choices about spending and saving, you're taking important steps toward financial empowerment!

The Possibilities Are Endless!

As you continue your journey through this book, remember that financial literacy is an ongoing process. Each chapter brings you closer to financial independence and success. Stay curious, stay motivated, and keep exploring the exciting world of finance and wealth-building!

Remember, you are the captain of your financial ship, and you now know how to make the most out of charting your own course to success. We've explored the currents of cash flow, the treasures hidden within budgeting, and the arts of savvy saving and spending. Whether you're starting with an allowance, hustling with a new online startup, or dreaming of financial independence, keep steering a straight course! The river may have plenty of twists and turns, but with the skills you've gained, you're ready to navigate towards the open waters of endless financial possibilities.

Better yet, there are more financial tips and tricks on the horizon! In the upcoming chapter, we'll unlock credit knowledge to give you a handy tool that will help you craft a financial reputation that will last a lifetime. You'll discover that credit isn't just about borrowing; it will help you achieve those significant milestones in your life – buying your first car, pursuing higher education, or starting a bigger business. Let's gear up for yet another valuable lesson in shaping your financial future for success!

6

The Credit Code

Lydia was so excited! She had just received an email confirmation that she was officially accepted to a special soccer camp in South America. It was a dream come true!

However, Lydia had a problem. She needed to pay for the plane ticket and quite a few travel supplies before her trip. She had successfully applied for and been granted a sports scholarship to pay for everything, but it looked like the funds would not be available for another three weeks! Lydia needed a strategy that allowed her to cover her immediate expenses and then pay them back as soon as her scholarship funds arrived.

This is where Lydia's student credit card came into play. While she still had a lot to learn about the credit system, she knew that this was the perfect time to use her available credit line on the card for her trip and then pay off the entire balance within 30 days to avoid fees or interest. Before making the purchases, Lydia did her research about when the scholarship money would arrive and talked to trusted people who gave her sound financial advice.

From there, she was confident that this was the right decision for her to make.

In this chapter, we're going to join Lydia and other young people as they discover the power of credit, learning the necessity of carefully planning ahead and staying on top of the details in any kind of borrowing situation. Let's get started!

 "The most important investment you can make is in yourself."

Warren Buffett

What is Credit?

Credit is an agreement between a creditor, or lender, and a borrower, or a debtor, where the lender gives the debtor funds for a certain amount of time. The debtor promises to repay the lender within the agreed-upon time along with a certain added percentage, or interest, or otherwise risk financial or legal penalties. Credit is not free money; it's trust, or the belief that you have the responsibility to return any borrowed money in the future.

Now, imagine that the early years of establishing credit provide you with the ability to prepare for the future. In that sense, credit is more than a tool for borrowing; it's a powerful ally in building trust and opening doors to financial expansion. Every time you use credit wisely, it contributes to the trust that money lenders have in you. On the other hand, if you do not carefully plan and manage your credit usage strategically, your financial reputation will diminish and many doors will be closed to you. When looked at as a whole, your credit transaction history tells a tale that contributes to the map of your financial journey. It goes beyond short-term gains to include long-term growth and building paths to diverse and rewarding destinations.

We'll talk more about credit opportunities and how your specific actions can establish either good credit or bad credit later on. For now, keep in mind that credit acts as a scorecard where each action leaves a mark, shaping your financial identity. It represents your financial reputation, reflecting not merely financial health but trustworthiness in all of your monetary interactions. The goal is to maintain good credit so you demonstrate a track record of reliability and sound decision-making, opening further opportunities to expand your financial leverage and wealth building.

 "An investment in knowledge pays the best interest."

Benjamin Franklin

The Cost of Using Credit

Back in Chapter 4, we already discussed interest when we went over the basics of banking, discovering how putting money into savings can earn you back pennies on the dollar. When using credit to borrow money, interest works in the other direction. Since the bank or credit company is putting their money into your hands, they expect a percentage back when you return it.

In that sense, depending on how you use it, credit can either be a helpful business partner or a dangerous enemy in your financial journey. Borrowing money comes with a definite cost! As if that is not enough, there's another twist—credit interest rates are extremely high because banks and credit companies want to make profits from your mistakes.

The credit system is designed to entice you in and give you difficult to understand information about the requirements because they hope to make a profit when you miss a payment or overuse your credit and cannot pay off the balance after the 30 day grace period.

The interest on your savings my be 3% but the interest on a credit card balance could be 24% or much higher! This will not only make it expensive and disheartening to give your hard earned money to a lender because you didnt have a plan, but using most or all of your credits card's limit will also make it harder for you to borrow in the future or maintain a good credit score. To avoid learning these things the hard way, read on to better understand how to remain diligent in your use of the credit system.

There is no limit to how much money I can make. I can earn money in both expected and unexpected ways.

The Truth About Credit Cards

Credit cards are powerful tools that are filled with both opportunities and risks. Let's follow Lydia as she plans to navigate the world with her first credit card and learn from her example.

Lydia is on a mission to prepare for summer soccer camp in South America. She knows exactly how much she can purchase with her card because she already has figured out how much money she is receiving from the scholarship, funds that she has already prepared to pay back the purchases as soon as the payment arrives.

Imagine walking beside her as she eyes the latest gaming console and those trendy sneakers everyone's talking about. The temptation is real! At first, Lydia feels it, too. But then she remembers her list and the purpose of her credit card. Instead of diving headfirst into impulse buys, she puts aside the desire for instant gratification and lets wisdom guide her choices. She uses her credit card as a strategic ally to move her comfortably forward on this next step of her summer journey.

Lydia sees her credit card as a teacher, not just a piece of plastic money. With every transaction, she is practicing a lesson in spending, saving, and strategic planning. Her long-term goal is to swipe with sense, distinguishing between her wants and her needs for her trip and making purchases that resonate with value and necessity.

As she continues to consider how credit will help her meet her financial goals, Lydia's adventures continue! She discovers the powerful habit of paying off her credit balance every month to keep her out of debt, free from high interest rates, and away from late fees.

Remember, credit is not free money. Using credit mirrors cash flow, which is to say that you should only make a purchase on a credit card if you have enough money in the bank to pay for it. As Lydia learns, during this stage in her life, using a credit card is an exercise in building a strong credit score to leverage wealth-building credit opportunities for the near future.

Now that we've brought the concept of credit score into the mix, let's take a look at what that's all about!

Your Credit Score

When you begin to operate with credit, you will develop something called a credit score that follows you around as your financial reputation. Think about it like a report card that shows whether or not you are trustworthy when it comes to borrowing and paying back money. Just like you want to have a good reputation among your friends and a great report card from school, you also want to have a solid credit reputation in the money world.

To keep an eye on your credit score and work on boosting it for the future, some apps like CreditKarma are a great resource. With their app you have free unlimited access to your score. Their app is designed to help you better understand your score and other financial topics. They market offers for credit cards, loans and other financial services as well so be smart about what you are really in the market for!

Why does having a credit score really matter? Here are a few reasons to think about, especially as you look to the future and seek financial independence:

- Buying and insuring a car: If you need a loan, lenders examine your credit score to determine if they are willing to give you money, and how much interest they will charge you when you pay back the loan.
- Paying for education: While applying for a federal college loan does not relate to your credit score, having good credit can help you qualify for better rates when applying for a private loan.
- Renting a house or apartment: Landlords are allowed to check credit scores before proceeding with your application, and they may even deny your application with a lower credit score.

- Applying for a job: Some employers check credit scores to see if you are reliable when it comes to paying bills before offering you a position.

Several different institutions called credit bureaus are behind your credit score — Experion, Equifax, and TransUnion. These groups monitor your score, keep track of your credit history, and penalize you every time you conduct certain credit activities.

For example, if you apply for a new credit card or miss a payment, the credit bureau will remove points from your score. Later on, we'll go over some tips on how to boost your credit score, but for now, just keep in mind all of the intricacies that go into this part of your financial journey and learn to pay the game!

"Abundance is not the absence of scarcity; it is the presence of abundant mentality."

Debasish Mridha

Interactive Element: The Tale of Two Approaches

To emphasize the facts about credit that we've already talked about, let's take a look at the financial journey of two 18-year-olds, Malik and Maeve. Through their examples, we'll better understand the importance of saving and using credit wisely instead of seeking every opportunity for instant gratification.

Like our friend Mateo who is a YouTube gamer, Malik and Maeve are two video game aficionados. They have been waiting for months for the hottest video game console to finally become available, and when it does, the price is $500.

In preparation for the console's release, Malik applied for a credit card earlier in the year and was approved for one with a $1000 limit and a 25% annual interest rate. Seeing the card as free money, Malik feels that he is simply not able to wait any longer and uses credit to buy the console.

Meanwhile, Maeve already has a credit card, too, but she has other plans for how it will benefit her financial journey in the future. The temptation is strong, but instead of taking a path of instant gratification, she decides to start by adding to her already growing savings. She sets aside a portion of her allowance every week, does extra chores, and even finds a weekend job at the local supermarket. Her desire for the console motivates her to work even harder, and she remains diligently focused on the prize as she devotes several months to obtaining the necessary funds.

When Maeve receives her package in the mail, she celebrates! She has worked hard, saved up, and bought a new console without any debt. In the process, she has learned valuable lessons about patience, hard work, and her money's real value.

Unfortunately, by the time Maeve is pulling her new console out of the box, Malik is experiencing financial challenges from his decision to treat his credit card like free money. The first month after the purchase, Malik receives a credit card statement with a minimum amount that he has to pay to escape being charged interest and additional fees. He ignores it, and by the time the second month's statement comes around, it shows that he not only owes the initial $500 but is also charged $10 interest! At that point, if he still doesn't pay anything, then the following month he will owe $510, more interest on top of that, and a late fee for missing a payment!

The worst part of Malik's situation is that he has not planned to make any payments, so he struggles to make it on time. In the end, he actually makes a late payment, which further damages his credit score. Malik learns that late payments are one of the hardest things to correct in his credit score because of the way the scoring model is weighted and how it takes years to diminish a late payment's negative effects. Just one or two late payments can affect his future attempts to get good insurance rates, auto loans, lease agreements, and property purchases!

Malik realizes the error of his ways by purchasing something on credit that he did not have the money for in the first place. He received his console right away, but he will end up paying too much for it in the long run. If he doesn't pay everything off soon, he will find himself tied to a small amount of debt that can create large consequences for his financial future.

As you reflect on the two different paths that these young gamers took, who do you think made the better choice? Why do you believe that? Are there any particular lessons that you can use for your own financial journey?

 "Don't let the fear of losing be greater than the excitement of winning."

Robert Kiyosaki

Mastering Student Credit Cards

Now let's talk about student credit cards for a bit. Ordinarily, credit companies make it difficult to obtain credit cards unless the applicant meets certain requirements. To get around this, many young people who are in a position to use a credit card will go the route of being an authorized user on their parent or guardian's credit account. This type of credit card is called a custodial account where the primary account holder is an adult and the young person is able to charge purchases to that card.

Students are able to obtain their own accounts under the right circumstances, and credit companies make those cards very attractive — offering an option that is easy to apply for, does not come with annual fees or income qualifications, and may even include rewards. This is so they obtain you as a customer early in life and then keep offering you more deals to remain with them long-term.

While this may sound good, the reality is that all good things in the credit world come with a catch. Like the card that Malik applied for, student credit cards often come with even higher interest rates than the standard card. As a result, if a student credit card carries a balance from month to month, the user will end up paying an incredible amount of interest!

When used responsibly, student credit cards are great for young adults learning to step into the realms of financial independence. They're not designed to be a tool for spending but a responsibility, an opportunity, and a stepping stone toward building a robust credit history. Navigating the journey with thoughtfulness means that a good credit score can cultivate a solid financial foundation that allows for greater borrowing power in the future.

Remember Jorge, our freshie in high school from Chapter 2? Some years later after he graduated, he started taking classes at a local college. To accompany his educational journey, Jorge obtained a student credit card – a key to new experiences and the financial autonomy he had always desired.

From the first week of orientation, Jorge felt exhilarated. The campus buzzed with life, and the thrill of newfound freedom surrounded him. He had many responsibilities to prepare for class, but he also was attracted to the swirl of activity around him – there were coffee shops to hang out in, concert tickets that friends were grabbing, and the latest tech gadgets guaranteed to give him an edge in learning.

Jorge realized that he faced a choice between necessity and desire. While he had a definite need to purchase food, supplies, and textbooks, other things pulled him in the direction of partying. Jorge had to make a firm decision not to indulge or go down the easy path of using his credit card now and thinking, "I can always pay it back later!"

In this challenge, Jorge intentionally practiced financial wisdom. He discerned the difference between his needs and wants, being responsible for covering the necessary items with his card and only indulging in a fun event or purchase when everything else had already been taken care of.

Like Jorge, many young people are forced to make a decision when they are in the middle of a situation. It is very easy to get tripped up in the moment and regret it later when stuck with interest, fees, and increasing rates. Jorge's example illustrates that self control, wisdom and responsibility go a very long way in the world of credit.

Interactive Element: Credit Card Tips and Commandments

Four Ways to Use a Credit Card to Build Your Credit Score:

1. Pay off your balance every month on time
2. If you have to carry a balance, keep your balance low, not more than 10% of the card limit
3. Limit the number of cards you open, one per year is best
4. Keep the same card for a long time

Five Common Mistakes When Using a Credit Card

1. Only paying the minimum instead of all or most of the balance
2. Loaning the card out to friends or family members
3. Using the card to pay for purchases that you cannot afford to pay for with cash
4. Applying for multiple credit cards at once
5. Canceling a credit card instead of using it occasionally

The Six Commandments of Owning a Credit Card

1. I will pay off my balance every month.
2. I will regularly monitor my activity.
3. I will not purchase things that I cannot afford.
4. I will plan my spending.
5. I will research my options and get rewarded with the best cashback offer and no annual fees.
6. I will never skip a payment.

For more, check out the free app called Credit Karma, which is a great resource to help you on your journey!

"What you get by achieving your goals is not as important as what you become by achieving your goals."

Zig Ziglar

From Credit Cards to Loans

Your financial voyage doesn't stop at the borders of credit card territories! It's time to set sail into uncharted waters where loans await your discovery, providing you with even greater financial opportunities. We'll get into discussing how certain things like your car, your laptop, or your particular skill set become treasured possessions that add value to the journey ahead.

First, let's talk about tangible assets – the things you own that have a physical form like your phone, bicycle, car, Xbox, and more. Everything you possess has value, and when you understand what each item is worth, it will help you make smarter decisions.

For example, suppose you have an old phone that you purchased several years ago for $100 that you want to trade in while buying a newer model that costs $500. Knowing the current value of your tangible asset, or your old device, is important when making the trade so that you experience a fair transaction.

As you grow older and begin thinking about making bigger purchases like a car or a house, understanding tangible assets is even more important because of the role they play in obtaining a loan or insurance policy.

The idea of tangible assets makes more sense when we think about them within the topic of loans. The definition of a loan is pretty basic – borrowing money with a promise to pay it back over time along with interest. Lenders prefer to only give loans for tangible assets because these things have a specific value. If a person takes out a loan and neglects to pay it back, the lender can take back the tangible asset, whether that means repossessing a car or foreclosing on a house.

Investing in Yourself With Loans

Now, let's think about the value of loans as a way to invest in yourself! Picture the concept of investment as sowing seeds in the garden of your future. Your education and the skills you nurture are like tiny, promising sprouts that push through the soil of life, seeking the sun of opportunity. With each new lesson and development of skill, you tend to your garden, nurturing it with the water of dedication and the fertilizer of hard work.

Investing in yourself is like building a masterpiece over time. While not all education opportunities require a loan, there are plenty of no or low cost courses and instruction available on any topic you can imagine these days! Should you decide that what you want to learn or who you want to learn from is just beyond your financial limits a loan can bridge that gap.

Every dollar or hour you spend on education and learning becomes a building block, constructing a bridge to new job opportunities, higher earnings, and personal development. The journey might not be easy, but it's a worthwhile quest to unlock the doors of your future! Remember, just like a credit card isn't free money, investing in yourself isn't giving money away but a downpayment on your growth, success, and next adventure still in the making.

So, how do loans play into this topic of investing in yourself? Let's join up with Sofia and learn how her journey plays out for a better understanding!

 I am proud of the person I am and the person I'm becoming. I am proud of myself and all that I have accomplished.

Sofia's Investment

Sofia has decided that it's time to expand her jewelry business by increasing her networking during the day and researching new ideas and business strategy at night. She's not just chasing her dreams, she's investing in them. Sofia is devoted to developing her skills, talents, and relational abilities – elements of what is known as "human capital."

Investing in human capital is like planting seeds in a personal garden of opportunities. Every hour Sofia dedicates to perfecting her craft, studying business, and learning from other artists means that she is strengthening herself and her creations. Her efforts are the nurturing waters that help her seedlings grow into a mighty tree.

As she pursues ways to expand her business, she dreams about renting a storefront so she has a physical location. She envisions a studio space that also allows her to showcase her products and expand her online presence. Sofia decides to explore her financial options. She discovers a connection with a reputable multi-million dollar business that helps young entrepreneurs by offering a small business loan for a certain length of time.

Sofia is faced with a critical choice. The idea of having a loan to achieve her dreams faster is incredible! Yet, taking on a loan is a massive responsibility that she is uncertain about paying back. She takes her time to research more options and gain the advice of trusted mentors.

In the end, Sofia's goals and dreams point her in the direction of taking that short-term loan to springboard her jewelry business from a small startup into a thriving career. Since she has already taken the time to develop her passion into a potential career path,

Sofia knows that she has the dedication to channel her creativity further and make a sustainable career doing what she loves most.

So, when Sofia has the opportunity to apply for this special small business loan, she sees it as a bridge to her dreams – a means to access the funds she needs to turn her creative vision into a reality! She is fully aware that loans come with a cost, but she is prepared to handle the responsibility of borrowing as her journey into the realm of loans begins.

The Reality of Loans

The reality is that loans are not freebies. When you take a loan, you're agreeing to pay back the money you borrowed along with interest. While loans can help you out, they come with an important task – paying them back. From the point of view of a lender, there is always a bit of risk involved when handing out cash. In that sense, interest is a small reward for allowing someone else to use their cash.

Sofia understands that taking the small business loan will be super helpful but needs to be handled wisely. As she continues to research what it means to be a small business owner, she digs into the world of responsible borrowing and makes it her mission to understand the fine print of her new loan.

Over time, Sofia makes her loan work to her advantage by using savvy strategies like keeping a close eye on her loan balance and the monthly interest rates. By staying on top of the details, she works out a specific plan to pay it back quicker without breaking the bank. This means making regular additional payments to chip away at the original amount Sofia borrowed, which is also known as the principle balance, lowering overall interest!

Sofia doesn't stop there! She considers more ways to slash interest costs. Sofia signs up for automatic payments because it includes a discount on interest rates. Every dollar that she saves on interest is a dollar closer to making her small business more profitable!

Sofia's story is proof that anyone who has the determination and financial know-how can turn a loan from a potential headache into a handy tool to obtain dreams. Through smart borrowing, careful planning, and a hunger for knowledge, Sofia not only gets her storefront but also expands to hiring artists to create in the studio and incorporates complementary products and custom services. She becomes so profitable that she is able to pay the loan back early and cover the rent for the storefront on her own by the third year! Sofia's journey to success is a prime example that you have the power to conquer any financial challenge that comes your way!

The World is Your Oyster

As we think back over the lessons we have covered about credit, interest, loans, and more, it solidifies the fact that the possibilities before each one of us in our individual financial journey are truly limitless! Every time we resolve to be responsible decision-makers when it comes to our money, we are setting ourselves up for financial success and additional rewards in the future.

Unlike Malik who used his credit card for immediate gratification, we can learn to be like Maeve who saw the opportunity to practice the values of patience, hard work, and savings before she fully enjoyed the fruit of her labor. As Sofia took a loan to invest in herself and in her small business, we are challenged to think outside the box and discover ways that we can pursue our dreams without breaking the bank!

In the following chapter, we will dive deeper into the concepts of interest and investments. This time, however, there is an added twist – we'll look at interest in a whole new way because of the power it can wield for us when given the advantage of time. From there, we'll take a look at different kinds of investments, further understanding how putting aside small amounts of income at the very beginning of our financial journeys will result in a tremendous return further down the road!

7

Small Steps Toward Investing for Big Rewards

Mateo was up late, surfing the web and chatting with some gamer buddies. He was specifically thinking about ways to grow his influence, strengthen his financial foundation, and prepare for the future.

Taking a look at some of the channels he followed, Mateo saw that a couple of gamers were also connected to someone named Sergei, so he started looking over those videos.

At first, Mateo felt a bit skeptical, seeing that all Sergei talked about was money growth. This was the real world, where money didn't grow on trees! Plus, Mateo didn't believe in anything that advertised itself as a "foolproof get rich quick" scheme, since those usually come with some kind of hidden subscription to a channel where some know-it-all-kid talked for hours about unverified material he found online.

Then Mateo ran across one video that talked about the importance of investing at an early age. Curious, he watched the whole thing and then jumped into the open video chat where a bunch of his friends and this new guy Sergei were talking.

"Does this really work?" was Mateo's first question.

"Let's take a look!" Sergei answered without hesitation, sharing his screen to show his personal investment account.

Over the next half-hour, Mateo gained a real education about the power of investing, and specifically how a few dollars put aside into certain funds over the course of many years yield big results in the future!

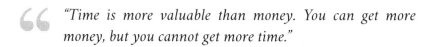

> "Time is more valuable than money. You can get more money, but you cannot get more time."
>
> Jim Rohn

In this chapter, we are going to explore the benefits of compound interest, which reveals how you can make small investments in your early years to reap a big reward by the time you reach retirement. Best of all, you will gain a better understanding of why starting your financial journey in your teens or early twenties is so important – because it grants you a huge advantage in wealth accumulation! Let's dive into the details of how to harness the financial superpower of investing and make it work for you.

The Power of Starting Early

In the last several chapters, we talked about two kinds of interest. Let's recap to refresh our memories. The first kind is our trusty friend, where we save money at a bank and earn a small percentage back. The second kind is a crafty foe because we are required to pay an additional percentage for borrowing money from a bank or credit institution. Both of these interest rates are known as simple interest because the percentage only applies to the principal amount.

Now, let's get deeper and talk about compound interest. At its core, compound interest is interest that is earned on top of interest! Think about it like planting a seed that grows into a tree, which in turn produces more seeds. Every one of these new seeds also grows into a tree, which multiplies your forest over time.

Since we are talking about increasing wealth instead of growing a tree farm, let's look at how compound interest can multiply your finances over time. Suppose you put $100 in a savings account that has a generous interest rate of 5%. At the end of the first year, your $100 gains $5 in interest and grows to a total of $105. This is an example of simple interest.

With compound interest, your interest growth shows an exciting twist – in the second year, you not only earn interest on your initial deposit of $100 but also on the additional $5 that came in at the end of the first year! Some accounts even calculate your interest according to month or quarter instead of waiting until the end of the year, which further increases the amount of interest that comes in! The longer you keep your money in this account, the more it continues to grow year after year. Even if you never add another penny, your money keeps working and growing for you!

I am grateful for the abundance that I have and the abundance that's on its way.

Now, you may be asking yourself, "So, what's the big deal with compound interest??" The whole point is to explore your options and tap into the power of financial growth over a long time. When you start early and have the patience for your money to grow over time, then you will be rewarded with a valuable nest egg that can provide for you far into retirement. In other words, as a young person, your financial superpower is time! The longer your money has to compound, the more you stand to gain.

Going back to the analogy of trees, there is an old Chinese proverb that says, "The best time to plant a tree was 20 years ago. The second best time is now." Think about that for a moment. Investing and gaining compound interest is a lot like how a tree grows. When you dedicate the time to plant an acorn or an apple seed today, your oak tree or apple tree will be that much taller, stronger, and more mature ten years from now than if you decide to wait until later!

Interactive Element: Predicting Growth

Online compound interest calculator:

https://www.nerdwallet.com/calculator/compound-interest-calculator

It's time to practice the magic of compound interest! By visualizing the actual way that your money grows over time, you will better understand how to take small, practical steps and make your finances work for you!

Step 1: Use your smartphone or tablet to scan the QR code that will take you to an online compound interest calculator.

Step 2: Start by entering these test numbers to see how your money will grow

- Initial deposit: $100
- Annual contribution: $100
- Interest rate: 5%
- Length of time: 50 years

Step 3: Now it's your turn! Think about your current budget and how much you will be able to contribute — both now and in the years to come. Can you see how your money grows over time and becomes something incredible?

The Basics of Investing

Let's check in with Maya and see what she is up to these days. She has been working hard at her part-time job along with her side hustles of babysitting and housesitting, diligently stacking cash in her savings account. While she enjoys the slow and steady financial growth where she lets it sit and earn a tiny amount of interest, it is not enough for her.

Maya starts looking into investing, an opportunity that gives her money a job where it will grow and multiply for her. Her long-term goal is to buy a house, so she wants to invest enough funds for a sizeable downpayment in the years to come. As she learns about all of the different investment options available to her, from stocks and bonds to real estate and collectibles, she searches for one that will give her real value to help her obtain her housing goal when she is ready to buy her own property!

Soon, Maya discovers a special feature that falls under one type of investment called the Roth IRA account. In this plan, she can open up an account under an investment platform like the standard full share brokerage like E*Trade, which requires you to invest in full shares so it cost more to get started or a fractional share micro-investing platform like M1 that allows you to invest what ever you have. She chooses to begin to make her contributions in a micro share platform so she can put any small or larger amounts to work right away. After five years of owning stocks, bonds, ETFs, and other types of investments, she will have the option to use those funds as a downpayment on her first home! She is excited about this, beginning to dive into opening up the Roth IRA and choosing the specific items she wants to invest in.

As Maya continues the investment process, she feels a sense of empowerment! She is asserting her agency, believing in herself as a financial decision-maker, and enjoying the fruit of her labor over time. She practices discipline, patience, and foresight – important habits that not only benefit her money matters but also strengthen her character.

Maya also understands that since she is beginning her investment journey at a young age, she is shaping her future, taking even more control over her path, and setting a foundation in place for financial freedom. Instead of following the traditional mindset of believing that she needs a large salary and substantial savings to cover the commissions when investing, Maya knows that modern platforms expand her options and remove those pesky commission fees to further benefit her in the long run.

Like Maya, you can also get started today on your investment journey! Just think: By setting aside just one dollar a day for the next twenty years, you can receive back up to $100,000. The secrets to these massive sums are compound interest and starting early to maximize your returns!

 "Investing puts money to work. The only reason to save money is to invest it."

Understanding Risks

Before we go further into explaining all of the different investment options that Maya was looking into, it's important to understand that there is a balance between risk and reward in every investment. We'll get into the different types of investment options in the next section, so as you do your own follow-up research, understand that certain kinds of investing lean toward a greater risk.

This is to say that the value of some items may suddenly drop, leaving you with a financial loss instead of a bigger payout. It is also possible that your investment item might drastically increase its value as well, giving you a tremendous reward! The uncertainty and unpredictability that go hand in hand with investing make for an ongoing adventure, requiring you to be willing to put in the constant work to explore which level of risk is right for you.

As Maya has already discovered, the potential risks to investing are often so great that they deter many people from investing in the first place! In fact, when Maya first investigated her options, she even temporarily decided to avoid investing altogether when she realized that she could possibly lose all of her rewards should the market suddenly make a shift in the wrong direction!

The fact that helped Maya change her mind was when she recognized that investing is like riding a seesaw — trying to find the proper balance between two sides. On one side, there's Reward and the potential for gain. On the other side, Risk stands ready for you to lose everything. Finding the right balance is key!

There are many examples of risk and reward in daily life. Consider, for instance, the risk you run in opening up your personal life to a completely new friend. On the one hand, they could turn out to be a great person, and you will have gained a new bestie. On the other hand, they could turn out to be manipulative and mean, using your personal information for their own benefit or laughing at you in front of other people.

When the stakes are high, it often means that the reward is high as well, but this is not always the case. For instance, you could run the risk of great loss because you chose something on a whim without doing your research. As we get into different investment options, keep in mind that it is important to determine what works for you and what is better left for someone else.

Choosing the Right Investment Vehicle

There are many different kinds of investment options to choose from. In the investment world, these are known as vehicles because they are a different way to carry your money and move it forward on a path to growth. The great thing is that every investment vehicle has its own perks, risks, and potential rewards. Let's explore each of your options below!

Stocks, Bonds, and More

Investing in stocks means that you are putting your money toward a specific company that you believe is in the process of growing and expanding. Essentially what you are doing when purchasing stock is buying a small piece of that company's earnings and assets, something called a share. Companies that have been around as long as you have or longer and pay dividends are a good place to start your long term investment plan. Dividends are profits from the company that are distributed to shareholders based on how many shares you own. You buy the stock, you become a shareholder. Dividends can be automatically reinvested in the purchase of more of the stock you already own which is better than compound interest!

Bonds are loans made to a major company, or more commonly to a government entity. When you purchase a bond, it is like putting your money into a savings account with a higher interest rate — you give the government a small loan and expect the bond issuer to borrow your money and pay you back with interest. Bonds are not as risky as stocks but they also do no have the potential to grow as much. Buying individual bonds may not be possible because of the expense and time you are required to hold the investment. The starter option is a mutual fund or index fund that holds lots of bonds.

Investing in mutual funds means that you are allowed to purchase a number of different investments all at once. You ordinarily have a professional manage the funds for a small fee so they can invest your money in groups of stocks, bonds, and other vehicles.

You may have heard of the S&P 500, Dow Jones or the Nasdaq, these are stock market indexes that contain certain high performing companies that investors follow to assess the health of the market. An index fund is a kind of investment that may include the companies in a particular index.

Then there is the type of index fund called the exchange-traded funds or ETFs. Essentially, ETFs follow a certain type of index fund and seek to duplicate its performance.

A certificate of deposit or CD is a savings account that earns compound interest at a higher interest rate than an ordinary bank account. It is set up for a fixed amount of time, like 12 months, 18 months, or even 5 years. When you open a CD, you are not permitted to touch the deposited funds until the allotted amount of time has expired, or you run the risk of paying a penalty.

A Roth IRA or individual retirement account that allows you to contribute as of this writing $6000 per year of your net earnings. (remember thats take home earnings after taxes are taken out) These earnings invested in your chosen investments grow tax free inside this account until retirement age or until the account is five years old, and used for a down payment on your first house!

Tangible Investments

Beyond the investments found in stocks, bonds, and CDs, there are tangible investments, or ones that you can see and touch. The first big one is real estate, the investment in a property since you hope that the value of the land and any improvements will steadily increase over the years. Also, if you rent out the house on a regular basis, you can earn additional income!

Real Estate Investment Trusts or REITs are a type of "real estate stocks." In this case, you buy shares into a company that owns large portions of real estate, which means that you get a piece of the income from real estate without having to actually purchase any property on your own.

If there are real estate stocks, there are real estate mutual funds, too. Called real estate funds, your invested money is managed by a professional along with other investors and used toward many different kinds of real estate opportunities for the greatest reward.

Collectibles, Art, Precious Metals, and More

Next, let's think about smaller tangible items. Collectibles are a popular investment because they can increase in value over time due to how rare that item may be. Some popular collectibles that can be a high demand item with an even higher price tag include comic books, antique toys, and clothes or shows that belonged to someone famous. If you can find a particular niche with an increasing demand, then you may find it rewarding to invest in that area!

Art is its own category and especially includes paintings and sculptures. For some, investing in art is more of a passion than an adventure to gain a higher return. The greater the fame of the artist, the more valuable their works can become.

Investing in gold, silver, precious stones or metals, and high-quality jewelry is another option. The more inflated a currency is, the more valuable such items become. Since many companies offer to sell and buy gold and silver, make sure you do your research ahead of time to make sure they are a reputable business and offer pure metals and stones.

Antique Cars And Other Vehicles

While it's a known fact that the value of a new car loses value as soon as it drives off the lot, antique vehicles are another story all together. Vehicles can be more than just an expensive item that gets you from one place to the next – they can also become assets that grow in value over time.

What separates regular vehicles from an antique? Consider a car, truck, or motorcycle that is rare, has a unique design, comes with a fascinating history, or is connected to a celebrity! Classic cars and collectible motorcycles in particular tend to appreciate over time, or increase their value, which makes them another investment choice.

Investing Digitally with Cryptocurrencies

With the rise of technology, let's take a look at two types of digital investment options. First, there are cryptocurrencies, or a digital currency that can be used for online purchases, exchanges on gaming platforms, or long-term investments. They operate by a technology known as blockchain, which is a tamper-resistant record of ownership and transactions.

Depending on the type of cryptocurrency, or crypto, that you buy into, it may be called a coin or token. Their name comes from cryptography, or the coding and ciphering techniques that keep them secure outside of an ordinary bank or government-regulated financial facility.

While you are most likely familiar with certain popular types of crypto — bitcoin, Ethereum, and dogecoin — there are actually over two million different cryptocurrencies in existence! Within that vast number, there is a wide range of valuations also, from popular and expensive types of the obscure and worthless ones. The world of online money is a bit like the wild west, some consider cryptocurrency more risky that stock market investments, so always pay attention and do your research ahead of time!

Another kind of invisible currency is the NFT, or non-fungible token, which is a digital number that designates the ownership of specific digital items like pictures, videos, and music. For example, if you own a physical piece of art, an original music recording, or another item, you can use an NFT to verify that you are the sole owner.

Once an item is designated as an NFT, you have the ability to sell or trade it to others — either directly or through actual auction houses at a physical location. The world of NFTs is ever growing and expanding, making it a potential investment option, especially when considering that some NFT artwork sells for millions of dollars!

Whatever type of investment vehicle you choose, remember the risk that is always associated with each one. While the reward is also there, be careful not to put all your investment eggs in one basket! Savings will always be the foundation of any smart investment plan. Holding on to those investments that you have deemed stable because they have been around awhile and will likely continue to hold their value or pay dividends is a good idea. As you diversify your assets across different vehicles, your potential for growth and real reward increases!

Micro-investing

Before closing out, let's see what Dean does as he navigates the world of early adulthood. While he does his research and has determined that he definitely wants to begin his own investment journey, his bills and expenses are adding up, making it difficult for him to see a way to regularly invest in his preferred vehicle while still making ends meet.

Fortunately, Dean is introduced to the power of micro-investing, which opens the door to a whole new opportunity! What is micro-investing? This is a method in which Dean can invest just a couple of dollars on a regular basis. He begins to think outside the box and realizes that all of the soft drinks he buys add up to $2.50 per day, which is $17.50 per week, and $75.00 a month!

Dean decides that as he sets aside his soda money every day and downloads an easy-to-use app, he is giving his money the chance to grow over time thanks to the magic of compound interest in the apps saving feature and using that savings to buy stocks and ETF's when he decides hes found one that satisfies his risk tolerance. He is satisfied that micro-investing is the way to go, not requiring him to invest huge sums of money but just a few dollars every day that will add up over time.

Another part that excites Dean is that his risk is relatively low because he is only investing a small amount. As a beginner, he has the opportunity to dip his toe into the investment landscape while still giving him control over his finances. As the months go by and he watches his soda money earn interest on his savings and dividends on his chosen investments and stock prices falling and rising back up, Dean feels a great sense of achievement and progress!

Interactive Element: Your Micro-Investment Journey

Now it's your turn! Based on what you've seen from Dean's example, take some time to see what could work for you.

1. Start with Research. Look into platforms that are set up to help you on your micro-investment journey. To get you started, check out M1, Acorn, and Stash. Some of these even allow you to open a Roth IRA if you are serious about your long term investment plan and need to start small.
2. Think Outside the Box. What fits into your budget? Can you set aside fifty cents, a dollar, or even more to get

started? Are withdrawals and selling investments easy if you need the cash?
3. Pick the Plan that Works for You! Based on your unique budget and the platform that resonates with your style, you're well on your way to start investing!

 "An investment in knowledge pays the best interest."

Benjamin Franklin

Small Steps, Big Wins

As we took a look at the different ways that compound interest, buying dividend stocks, and other investments work and how investing your finances consistently today will turn into large sums in the future, let this knowledge motivate and excite you about the possibilities for your own life!

Take some time to think about what steps you can take — right now! — to invest in your future. Whether you are like Maya who dives into the realm of stocks by opening a Roth IRA or Dean who sets his daily beverage money for microinvesting, your small decisions now will reap a big reward by the time you reach retirement! Plus, even though retirement may sound like a world apart for when you are in your 60s and 70s, setting yourself up for financial success by making great decisions today means that you can retire from a career in your 40s and 50s so you can spend more time with the people and things that you love.

A big part of the thought process that goes into investment requires you to be forward-thinking. This may be very challenging to do, especially when so much is going on today in your day-today life! To help face this difficulty, the next chapter is going to talk about the importance of dreams and goals. You will learn the importance of aligning your financial goals with your greatest values, which will provide you with a deep and satisfying path to success! Are you ready?

8

Unlocking the Future

Clara had a dream. When we first met her back in Chapter 2, she had just begun looking for a part-time job so she could buy a tablet. Her goal at that time was to stay organized as she navigated activities at school, her drama team, and the community theater, building experience for her future.

Now, it's the start of a new school year and all Clara can think about is graduating so she can open up her own studio, hold drama classes, and direct real theater productions!

The only problem with her dream, however, is that she doesn't have a plan to move it forward and make it work.

In fact, when friends hear her talk about her dream, they ask, "How are you going to do that with the community theater being so big?" and "What's your plan to make it work?"

Clara doesn't have clear answers at this point, so she just says, "Wait and see!"

While Clara is very optimistic about her dreams, it is very important for us to take the time in this chapter to make a distinction between dreams and goals. As we delve into the details, you'll not only learn how to align your financial goals with existing values but also grasp why this connection is so critical in creating your own authentic and satisfying path to success. In other words, it's time to transform your dreams into value-driven game plans!

 "A dream written down with a date becomes a goal. A goal broken down into steps becomes a plan. A plan backed by action makes your dreams come true."

Greg Reid

Dreams vs. Goals

Let's start by defining our terms. What is a dream, what is a goal, and what makes the difference between them so important? Simply put, while a dream is a future outcome, a goal is a future action. Dreams can be endless with no specific timeline or destination in sight, but every goal comes with specific deadlines.

Then there is the cost aspect where time, money, and hard work are involved. Your goals come with a cost, which varies according to the type of goal you are setting for yourself. Dreams, however, are completely free!

At the end of the day, the primary difference between dreams and goals is the end result. Goals are reached when you focus on a specific result and meet it, working tirelessly to expand yourself and your capabilities. Dreams are vague, carrying you and your imagination along endlessly, but never reaching a specific destination.

At this point, you may be tempted to conclude that while dreams may be fun, they have no great purpose in comparison to goals. Not so! In the ideal situation, dreams and goals work hand in hand to get you where you want to go. How will you know what financial goals you want to reach without an initial dream to get you started?

Goals anchor dreams with purpose and direction. So, start every journey by dreaming big, and then pair those amazing dreams with clear, actionable financial goals to make the real magic happen! Goals are what take you from wishing to winning.

 "Believe you can and you're halfway there."

Theodore Roosevelt

Interactive Element: Finding Help with Planning Your Future

As you think about your future, certain parts of it may seem overwhelming because you have never been down this path before. That's perfectly okay! One of the best things about life is that there are many people around us who we can bounce ideas off of, take advice from, and share the journey with. In fact, chances are that if you have a dream to do something or be someone specific, there's someone else who has taken that path ahead of you!

To help you get started, it's often helpful to find a friend who can encourage you as you make the transition from dreamer to goal-setter and goal-achiever. This friend can be your age or an adult, but look for someone who is there to offer advice and be a sounding board, but will leave the decision-making process up to you.

Whether it is a best friend, friend of a friend, parent, guardian, teacher, sports coach, or friend's parent, think about asking someone to be there for you as you take the next steps forward. You can even ask them specifically to be your mentor as you move forward.

Here are some questions that you can ask them to get things started:

- How do I narrow my focus? I have so many ideas, but I know that I can only do so much!
- How do I face failure? When is it okay to mess up, and when it is a real problem?
- How do I deal with the things that I don't know yet? How can I make decisions when I don't know my options and don't know how to accept the unknowns?

Mapping Out Your Goals

Now let's get into what it looks like to move from dreams to goals with realistic results! Your financial dreams can include ideas like, "I want to be independent," and "I want to make my own decisions about my clothes, weekend plans, education and training, and more." As you apply certain principles to your dreams to turn them into financial goals, you will gain more and more control over your future!

In fact, setting financial goals is a big part of planning for your future. Whether you're focused on starting a business, attending college, buying a car, or taking a cool vacation with friends, knowing where you're currently at financially helps you know how to adjust your actions and reach where you need to be to obtain your current focus. Making specific decisions helps your dreams move from the category of "I'll do this someday..." to the place where you confidently say, "I'm doing it!

A financial goal may be either long-term or short-term, depending on your target. For example, if you want to take a cool vacation with friends next month, your financial steps to reach this short-term goal will be much different than the long-term steps you put in place to buy a house or obtain your master's degree.

Remember Dean? He is currently operating very successfully as an artist and graphic designer while managing his own Etsy shop, but he aspires to broaden his horizons and explore his possibilities. Instead of taking the traditional route of pursuing a degree in art, he feels that he is already immersed in the real-life practice of art and wants the chance to look into more opportunities. His big dream is to take some time to visit several cities around the world that specialize in art – Paris, France; New York City, USA; and Florence, Italy – before settling down in his own apartment and experimenting to further develop his unique style.

To reach both his long-term and short-term goals, Dean begins to reflect on his values. We already talked about financial values in Chapter 4 and how they serve as a compass to help you decide what you want to spend your money on. In the same way, your values help define and solidify your financial goals!

Ask yourself, "What truly matters to me?" This could be things like friendship, creativity, adventure, or compassion. Knowing what you stand for helps you make decisions that feel right. Let's walk with Dean through his values to better understand how they serve his financial goals. As you read through this, go ahead and imagine how the same value can serve your goals as well!

Authenticity

Dean wants to be true to himself above all. When his financial goals mirror his value of authenticity, he is not just following the crowd or being swayed by what everyone else is doing; he's making decisions that feel genuine and true to who he is.

Commitment

If Dean knows anything about goals, it's this simple fact – when someone truly believes in something or cares deeply about it, they're more likely to stick with it! As he begins to save money for his future art adventure, Dean knows that it will be easier to remain motivated and stay on track because he has been longing to make this trip for several years.

Personal Fulfillment

As Dean works to achieve his goals, he doesn't only feel a sense of financial satisfaction every time he takes a look at his savings account. He also feels a sense of deeper personal fulfillment because his goals truly resonate with who he is.

Meaningful Impact

Another value that is close to Dean's heart is that all of his goals and decisions make a meaningful impact. For some people, this might mean supporting sustainable businesses, donating to charities, or investing in education. For Dean, he longs to enjoy more beautiful art, so his financial choices reflect this wish that he wants to see and contribute throughout the world.

Avoiding Regrets

Dean wants to avoid living a life of regret, so he steers clear of spending his hard-earned money on fleeting trends or items driven by peer pressure. As he learns how to align his spending and saving with his core beliefs, he cherishes the choices he has made and feels a sense of satisfaction and meaning.

Transforming Dreams into SMART Goals

Now that you've seen a practical explanation of what it means to match goals with values, it's time to get into the exciting stuff – making your goals happen! It begins by lining up your dreams with goals that are SMART. What does it mean to create SMART goals? We touched on this in an earlier chapter, but it's time to dive in deep and get to the core of the matter.

SMART is an acronym for five powerful words – Specific, Measurable, Achievable, Relevant, and Time-bound. The practice of evaluating and implementing SMART goals started in psychology studies, showing that people perform better when using these measurements in their own lives. Let's continue to follow Dean on his journey as we walk through each step below.

Specific

What do you want to accomplish in order to reach the financial goal inspired by your dreams? Start being SMART by pinpointing your goals as much as possible. When you are vague, your goals will be too, and it will be that much more difficult to reach a result. When you are clear and your goals are specific, it will be easy to execute. Ask yourself the "Who?" "What?" "Where?" "When?" "Why?" and "How?" questions, such as "How much money do I want to make?" "When am I going to make it?" "What financial freedom will I enjoy as a result? Feel free to add other questions to help narrow down your answers!

In Dean's preparation for his great art adventure, his first specific goal is to save up for a high-powered camera. His plan is to gain a clear advantage in making his design dreams a reality by having the right equipment.

Measurable

For a goal to be measurable, it means that you are able to set a precise timeline with a deadline that is carefully marked down on your calendar. If your goal is not able to be measured, you will face uncertainty and possibly even repeated failure. For every goal that comes with a precise timeline, you will be able to track your progress, feeling motivated and empowered as a result. Best of all, once you meet your deadline, you will feel an even greater sense of satisfaction and accomplishment!

How does Dean make his goal to purchase a camera measurable? First, he sits down and calculates how much he needs to save each month to have enough for the camera of his choice. Then, he puts a hard date on his calendar to check his savings account and, if all goes according to plan, put in his order!

Achievable

SMART goals are realistic, requiring you to be honest with yourself and with others about your abilities. Why set a goal for yourself that you are not even able to meet? It will only serve to frustrate yourself and disappoint others. As you set and meet achievable financial goals, it will further inspire you to keep pushing for greater possibilities!

Dean knows that his short-term goal to purchase a great camera is a realistic one. Not only does he have the reliable income to save up enough for his big buy, he also has reliable friends who are experts in technology and will help him pick the exact camera model that will serve his needs.

Relevant

Guaranteeing that a goal is relevant goes back to the discussion about alignment with values. Does your financial goal resonate with you, or are you simply aiming toward it because someone said you should, or you just thought it was the latest thing to do? It is also important to consider your personal abilities and current path in life. For example, you may have a goal to save for that masters degree because you really want that certification, but it is not a relevant goal until you have your bachelors!

In Dean's case, he knows that his goal to buy a camera is relevant to his values and long-term plans. Making the purchase will give him the incentive to capture inspirational photos and further provide him with the motivation to let his imagination for art and design flourish!

Time-Bound

Let's go back to thinking about the goal being measurable because of the timeline that is attached to it. In the same way, your financial goal needs to be limited by a certain amount of time to remain fresh, inspiring, and active. Otherwise, it will easily stagnate and you will need to revisit whether or not your goals are actually SMART!

Because Dean's purchase date is on his calendar, he knows that this short-term goal is bound by a timeline. As the clock continues to tick and his savings account collects the necessary funds, Dean becomes more excited about the date that is just around the corner. With this dedication and focus, there is no chance that his goal to buy a camera will stagnate!

Interactive Element: Dream to SMART Goal Converter

With your deeper understanding of how SMART goals work, it's time to make the magic happen! This converter will walk you through the practical steps of turning your dreams into a solid game plan that reflect who you are and what you value.

Step 1: Dream Big!

Before anything else, let your imagination roam. Think about your wildest dreams and desires. Do you want to travel? Launch a YouTube channel? Buy a guitar? Jot it all down. Dreams are your starting point, not the destination.

Now, out of all of those dreams that you thought of, pick one that you'd really love to work on right now. It doesn't have to be the biggest one, but it certainly can be!

Step 2: Convert Your Dream!

Now it's time to turn your dream into a SMART goal using the five values below. For each set of questions, be as detailed as possible.

> **S - Specific:** What exactly do you want to achieve?
> **M - Measurable:** How will you know you've achieved it? How much money will be in your account? Or, what will the clear outcome be?
> **A - Achievable:** Is this a realistic goal given your current

resources and constraints? How can you and you alone make it happen?

R - Relevant: How does this goal align with your values and bigger life plans?

T - Time-bound: When do you aim to achieve this goal? What is your clear deadline?

Step 3: Break It Down!

Now that you have aligned your dream with your deepest values, it's time to take it a step further by listing three smaller actions that will help you begin to move toward your SMART goal.

Got that big dream in sight? Awesome! Now, break it down into smaller, manageable chunks. Using Dean's example of taking his art adventure around the world, here's how to break his goal into smaller, manageable chunks:

> **A. Research:** Learn about the best cities to visit that are known art hotspots. Explore budgeting tips through books, blogs, and YouTube videos.
>
> **B. Save up:** Set up a dedicated savings account called Dean's Art Adventure. Break down the total cost into smaller monthly or weekly contributions.
>
> **C. Map it out:** Create a rough itinerary to keep the dream on track. For foreign countries, master a few essential phrases in the respective languages.
>
> **D. Budget:** Create an overall budget for the trip, including accommodations, transportation, meals, and activities. Then break that down according to city.

Step 4: Visualize Success!

It's time to visualize meeting your goals! How does it feel to imagine that you have achieved what you set out to accomplish? Draw a picture or write an explanation to share your feelings when reading over your milestones! Does this further motivate you to keep focused?

Step 5: Share Your Plan!

Talk about your goals with friends and family. Not only can they offer support and advice, but they might even share the same dreams and your SMART actions may even motivate them!

"You can only become truly accomplished at something you love. Don't make money your goal. Instead, pursue the things you love doing, and then do them so well that people can't take their eyes off you."

Maya Angelou

Bonus Interactive Element: The Ultimate Vision Board

As a bonus, create your personalized Ultimate Vision Board with images and quotes, setting it in a place where you and others will see it. It will help you make financial planning more tangible and exciting. By visualizing your goals, you'll be more motivated to achieve them and more aware of the steps that you need to take.

Take a look at the following steps that will help you embrace your goals, stay on track, recognize your mistakes, and celebrate your successes. It may even inspire others!

Step 1: Affirm Your Journey

Write a personal affirmation that will guide your mindset moving forward. For example: "I am in control of my financial future and every step I take brings me closer to my dreams."

Step 2: Value Check

Pull your core values from the activity you did in Chapter 4. List them in the first column. Remember, these are your guiding principles. They'll help you make decisions that resonate with your true self.

Step 3: Dream Big

List all your dreams. Let them flow! Ask yourself: "Do my dreams reflect my values?" Emphasize the ones that you can start converting into SMART goals right away.

Step 4: Break It Down

Transform those dreams into something actionable by going through the SMART converter. What steps do you need to take to make them real?

Step 4: Fund Your Dreams

How do you plan to earn the money for these goals – a job, a cool side hustle, or maybe an entrepreneurial venture? Dive back into Chapter 3 if you need ideas!

Step 5: Power-Up

List three resources or people you can learn from for each dream turned into SMART goal.

Step 6: Vibe with Your Vision

Start collecting images, quotes, and symbols that resonate with your dreams, goals, and values. These could be cut out from magazines, printed, or handdrawn. Can you see how everything is coming together?

Step 7: Reflection

Take a step back and reflect on the process of creating your vision board. How did it make you feel? Do your goals feel more tangible now? What did you discover about your financial dreams and yourself?

This vision board serves as a powerful bridge between your dreams and your long-term financial success and prosperity. It acts as a constant reminder of the big picture so you can be motivated to make financial decisions that align with your vision. Stay focused and keep moving forward!

More important than the how we achieve financial freedom, is the why. Find your reasons why you want to be free and wealthy."

Robert Kiyosaki

Share Your Success!

I can't wait to hear about your successes – and the best part is that when you leave them online, you'll inspire other young people to whip their financial literacy into shape too.

Simply by sharing your honest opinion of this book and a little about your financial journey so far, you'll show new readers exactly where they can find this essential guidance.

Thank you so much for your support. I can't wait to hear from you!

Scan the QR code for a quick review!

Conclusion

Congratulations! You have successfully reached the end of our journey, for now! We're back where we started – it's time to check in and see where our money mindset has landed us.

Are you feeling pumped and energized by the wealth of information you just received? Or are you a little overwhelmed and disheartened because it looks like so much hard work lies between you and your dreams? Remember, everything begins with the mindset, so stay positive, take one step at a time, this is a marathon not a sprint, and you will go far!

Now, let's reflect on the places that we have been together and what they mean for your financial freedom. First, we started by learning how to handle personal finances – the power of a growth mindset, the diverse avenues of earning money, and how side hustles can morph into fulfilling careers.

From there, we examined the tricks of the trade in modern banking and making the most out of charting your own course to success. We explored the currents of cash flow, the hidden treasures of budgeting, and the balance between savvy saving and smart spending. Even though the river of life includes plenty of twists and turns, the skills gained prepared you to navigate the open waters toward endless financial possibilities.

Then there was the credit system, filled with many twists and turns, paths and pitfalls that can easily result in failure instead of success. By navigating it carefully with the right kind of perspective driven by knowledge, you will be able to have your credit score work in your favor rather than being drowned by the craftiness of the system.

Finally, as we explored the many possibilities of investment, you saw that it is not necessary to overwhelm yourself by feeling like you have to choose the perfect investment vehicle. Rather, the journey can be as simple as giving up your soda money every day to prepare for a rich future. We brought it all back together by making a distinction between dreams and goals, understanding that the connection between values and plans is critical to laying an authentic and satisfying path to success.

Now, can you imagine how these lessons will play out in real-life situations? Think past the details of opening a savings account or applying for your first credit card to some of the deeper subjects of investment and goal-setting. Have you thought about sustaining yourself through an online gig or setting yourself up for early retirement? If you haven't already realized, the time to start preparing for the far-off future is today – and the possibilities are all within your reach!

So, just how do you continue your momentum toward success? For starters, remember that the knowledge you have gained is not money theory – it is practical and highly applicable to your daily life. Also, continuing to educate yourself about financial matters is crucial. While our journey has already been jam-packed with details that will serve you well for the rest of your life, there are other higher-level money management strategies waiting for you just around the corner – from owning property and valuable assets to paying off both short-term and long-term debt, and more!

Remember, even though this book is coming to a close, your journey is just getting started! As you follow the steps in this book and find your unique treasure chest, we would love to hear from you. Scan the code to drop a review and tell us what your success story looks like. The adventure continues!

Resources

Free Gift 6 resume templates:
https://www.canva.com/design/DAF8DMB9_fY/2cm6lVALZWvR6hIkamMQAA/edit?utm_content=DAF8DMB9_fY&utm_campaign=designshare&utm_medium=link2&utm_source=sharebutton

Resume Builder:
https://www.myperfectresume.com/build-resume/mobile/choose-template

Job Activity Sheet:
https://www.twinkl.com.ph/resource/cfe2-p-71-my-ideal-job-activity-sheet

Student Accounts:

- Wells Fargo – Teen Checking: https://www.wellsfargo.com/checking/student/

- Bank of America – Student Banking: https://www.bankofamerica.com/student-banking/

- Chase – First Banking: https://personal.chase.com/personal/first-banking

- Capital One – Kids Savings Account: https://www.capitalone.com/bank/savings-accounts/kids-savings-account/

- PNC Bank – PNC 'S' is for Savings: https://www.pnc.com/en/personal-banking/banking/savings/s-is-for-savings.html

- TD Bank – TD Simple Savings: https://www.td.com/us/en/personal-banking/savings-accounts/simple

Free Credit Score App:
http://creditkarma.com

References

Berger, Rob. "Top 100 Money Quotes of All Time." Forbes. Last modified April 30, 2014. https://www.forbes.com/sites/robertberger/2014/04/30/top-100-money-quotes-of-all-time/?sh=3feaf8344998

https://www.verywellfamily.com/a-teen-slang-dictionary-2610994

https://www.goodreads.com/quotes/971771-the-mind-is-everything-what-you-think-you-become

https://www.verywellmind.com/what-is-a-mindset-2795025

https://schools.au.reachout.com/articles/mindsets

https://www.linkedin.com/pulse/psychology-money-mindset-how-your-beliefs-affect-financial-singh

https://www.linkedin.com/pulse/how-your-mindset-impacts-finances-finvision-financial-services

https://powerforwardgroup.com/blog/your-money-mindset

https://bethebudget.com/money-and-your-mind

https://www.psychologytoday.com/us/blog/mental-wealth/202108/how-your-parents-beliefs-about-money-affect-you

https://missionwealth.com/inspired_living_post/did-you-inherit-your-beliefs-about-money-from-your-parents

https://accruentadvisors.com/do-we-inherit-money-beliefs-from-our-parents

https://www.linkedin.com/pulse/top-7-limiting-beliefs-around-moneywhich-one-yours-marisa-punshon

https://www.thefinancialfairytales.com/blog/10-limiting-beliefs-about-money

https://static1.squarespace.com/static/5ef12bcfddbf393489fa98bc/t/5f6d58e5e1cc3618a88ca2a0/1601001701699/money_mindset_wkst.pdf

https://financeoverfifty.com/money-journaling-prompts

https://www.intelligentchange.com/blogs/read/free-yourself-from-old-narratives-and-write-a-new-one

https://www.psychologytoday.com/us/blog/quantum-leaps/201907/how-rewrite-your-past-narrative

https://www.chantellegrady.com/journal/2020/8/12/letting-go-of-your-old-stories

https://thehealthsessions.com/narrative-psychology-how-to-rewrite-your-life-story

https://www.cbsnews.com/news/bruno-mars-used-to-call-home-60-minutes

https://www.staradvertiser.com/2016/11/17/features/bruno-mars-talks-to-60-minutes-about-childhood-in-hawaii

https://economictimes.indiatimes.com/magazines/panache/from-an-impoverished-single-mom-to-worlds-richest-writer-a-look-at-jk-rowlings-incredible-journey/living-on-welfare/slideshow/102276495.cms

https://www.biography.com/authors-writers/jk-rowling-harry-potter-author-rags-to-riches-billionaire

https://kidshealth.org/en/teens/gratitude.html

https://www.sagespring.com/4-ways-gratitude-can-improve-your-money-mindset

https://prowealthinvest.com/blog/what-gratitude-can-teach-you-about-money

https://www.happierhuman.com/gratitude-prompts-teens

https://www.azquotes.com/quote/527418

https://www.kidsmoney.org/parents/money-management/banking

https://www.forbes.com/advisor/banking/how-do-banks-work

https://www.investopedia.com/terms/b/bank.asp

https://www.easypeasyfinance.com/what-is-a-bank-for-kids-students

https://www.chase.com/personal/banking/education/basics/can-a-teenager-open-a-bank-account

https://www.thebalancemoney.com/types-of-bank-accounts-315458

https://www.nerdwallet.com/article/banking/checking-vs-savings

https://www.investopedia.com/checking-vs-savings-accounts-4783514

https://www.wisebread.com/6-important-things-to-look-for-in-a-savings-account

https://www.kotak.com/en/knowledge-centre/key-factors-to-consider-when-opening-a-savings-account.html

https://www.alliantcreditunion.org/money-mentor/what-to-look-for-in-a-savings-account

https://www.cnbc.com/select/how-to-choose-checking-account

https://www.military.com/paycheck-chronicles/2011/02/01/ten-things-to-consider-when-choosing-a-bank-or-credit-union

https://www.investopedia.com/best-student-bank-accounts-4799707

https://investinganswers.com/articles/checking-vs-savings-accounts

https://getschooled.com/article/5536-checking-vs-savings

https://www.forbes.com/advisor/banking/what-is-digital-banking

https://www.forbes.com/advisor/banking/benefits-of-digital-banking

https://youngandtheinvested.com/banking-apps-for-kids-and-teens

https://www.doughroller.net/personal-finance/budgeting/best-money-apps-for-kids-teens-and-young-adults

https://www.fool.com/the-ascent/banks/best-banking-apps

References

https://www.bankrate.com/banking/what-is-a-digital-wallet
https://www.investopedia.com/terms/d/digital-wallet.asp
https://geniusee.com/single-blog/top-digital-wallets-you-need-to-know
https://stripe.com/resources/more/digital-wallets-101
https://plumpos.com/digital-wallet.html
https://www.bankaroo.com/the-top-6-things-your-child-should-know-about-banking
https://due.com/banks-arent-your-friends
https://www.mywealthplanners.com/2021/07/20/banks-are-not-your-friend
https://n26.com/en-eu/blog/hidden-fees-in-banking-to-be-aware-of
https://amberstudent.com/blog/post/top-hidden-bank-account-charges-and-how-to-avoid-them
https://www.investopedia.com/decentralized-finance-defi-5113835
https://www.coinbase.com/learn/crypto-basics/what-is-defi
https://www.goodreads.com/quotes/7462032-opportunities-don-t-happen-you-create-them
https://kcparent.com/parenting/nine-lessons-teens-learn-from-having-a-job
https://amberstudent.com/blog/post/10-benefits-of-a-part-time-job-as-a-student
https://medium.com/@fniazi201276/unleashing-the-power-of-earning-the-key-to-personal-empowerment-and-fulfillment-74a0e19220c8
https://www.inclusion-europe.eu/having-job-means-having-freedom-to-make-your-own-choices-and-to-control-your-own-life
https://www.monster.com/career-advice/article/teen-jobs-0617
https://www.indeed.com/career-advice/finding-a-job/best-jobs-for-teens
https://www.thebalancemoney.com/tips-for-getting-your-first-part-time-job-2058650
https://www.thebalancemoney.com/teens-and-income-taxes-2610240
https://files.consumerfinance.gov/f/documents/cfpb_parents_pay-stub-activity.pdf
https://www.adp.com/resources/articles-and-insights/articles/g/gross-pay-vs-net-pay.aspx
https://www.taxslayer.com/blog/teen-filing-first-tax-return/
https://thesoccermomblog.com/ideal-job-worksheet-free-printable
https://www.teacherspayteachers.com/Product/My-Dream-Job-3173050?st=7141e17b54ecc72c0f613100e4ff3f73
https://www.twinkl.com.ph/resource/cfe2-p-71-my-ideal-job-activity-sheet
https://retailsolutions.ie/blog/entrepreneurship-8-advantages-to-being-your-own-boss

References

https://www.indeed.com/career-advice/finding-a-job/advantages-entrepreneurship
https://www.leangap.org/articles/4-benefits-of-starting-a-business-as-a-teenager
https://www.linkedin.com/pulse/building-your-future-how-entrepreneurship-can-lead-wealth-abhi-golhar
https://www.abovethecanopy.us/entrepreneurship-as-a-means-to-financial-independence
https://www.incfile.com/start-a-business/teen-business
https://greyjournal.net/hustle/inspire/top-10-teen-entrepreneurs-to-watch-in-2020
https://www.indeed.com/career-advice/finding-a-job/what-is-side-hustle
https://ayara.co/why-every-student-should-have-a-side-hustle
https://www.modakmakers.com/blog/the-benefits-of-having-a-side-hustle
https://www.nichepursuits.com/weird-ways-to-make-money-online
https://bloggingguide.com/how-to-sell-canva-templates-on-etsy
https://roadlesstraveledfinance.com/get-paid-chat-english
https://www.thewaystowealth.com/make-money/creative-ways-to-make-money
https://kingged.com/get-paid-to-write-subtitles
https://yourlifestylebusiness.com/low-content-books
https://www.crowdspring.com/blog/side-hustle-branding
https://www.linkedin.com/pulse/3-reasons-why-you-should-brand-your-side-hustle-mark-powers
https://www.skillshare.com/en/blog/branding-your-side-hustle
https://www.goodreads.com/quotes/258944-it-s-not-your-salary-that-makes-you-rich-it-s-your
https://nicolasboucher.online/2023/04/11/cash-flow-explained-to-kids
https://www.experian.com/blogs/ask-experian/what-is-cash-flow
https://www.thebalancemoney.com/how-to-separate-wants-and-needs-453592
https://www.linkedin.com/pulse/mindful-spending-heart-financial-wellness-quatriz
https://www.calstate.edu/csu-system/news/Pages/Money-Can-Make-You-Happier-If-You-Spend-it-Right.aspx
https://www.linkedin.com/pulse/breaking-free-from-comparison-trap-why-its-time-embrace-tony-fahkry
https://therapychanges.com/blog/2022/04/mirror-mirror-breaking-free-of-the-comparison-trap
https://jamesclear.com/core-values
https://www.discover.com/online-banking/banking-topics/3-reasons-to-save-more-money
https://www.mybanktracker.com/blog/find-my-answers/freedom-fund-259615

https://www.morty.com/resources/money-matters/the-key-to-make-savings-fun-the-freedom-fund

https://www.comparethemarket.com/meerkat-your-life/articles/whats-a-freedom-fund-and-why-do-we-all-need-one

https://www.junofunds.co.nz/You-Money/You-Money-Article/why-you-need-a-freedom-fund

https://www.mydoh.ca/learn/money-101/money-basics/why-kids-and-teens-should-start-saving-money-early

https://www.nerdwallet.com/article/finance/what-is-a-budget

https://www.linkedin.com/posts/hannah-greenwood-57a1b681_budgeting-is-not-about-depriving-yourself-activity-7051472417021403137-XuR-

https://www.experian.com/blogs/ask-experian/budget-mistakes-to-avoid/#s5

https://www.refinery29.com/en-us/how-to-make-budgeting-fun

https://herestudents.com/news/how-to-make-budgeting-fun

https://pplprs.co.uk/health-wellbeing/music-reduce-stress/

https://www.cnbc.com/select/no-spend-challenge

https://www.centralbank.net/learning-center/a-no-spend-month-can-help-you-save

https://www.afarber.com/blog/how-to-determine-if-an-expense-is-worth-it

https://www.goodreads.com/quotes/5205902-the-most-important-investment-you-can-make-is-in-yourself

https://www.gohenry.com/us/blog/financial-education/teaching-kids-about-credit-in-simple-terms

https://www.gohenry.com/us/blog/financial-education/what-is-interest-explaining-to-your-kids-in-simple-terms

https://www.forbes.com/advisor/credit-cards/average-credit-card-interest-rate/

https://www.nerdwallet.com/article/finance/credit-score-ranges-and-how-to-improve

https://www.hsbc.com.ph/credit-cards/credit-score

https://www.experian.com/blogs/ask-experian/why-is-credit-important

https://www.nerdwallet.com/article/finance/what-is-credit

https://www.nerdwallet.com/article/finance/credit-score-employer-checking

https://www.bankrate.com/personal-finance/credit/the-high-cost-of-a-low-credit-score

https://www.experian.com/blogs/ask-experian/can-my-credit-score-affect-renting

https://www.cnbc.com/2020/12/17/poor-credit-scores-affect-more-than-just-getting-a-loan-or-credit-card.html

https://www.moneyhelper.org.uk/en/everyday-money/types-of-credit/simple-

guide-to-credit-cards
https://www.fool.com/the-ascent/credit-cards/how-get-credit-card-for-student-no-income
https://www.investopedia.com/should-i-get-a-student-credit-card-5192378
https://www.fool.com/the-ascent/credit-cards/articles/5-mistakes-young-adults-make-first-credit-cards
https://www.myhonorbank.com/blog/how-to-use-a-credit-card-responsibly
https://www.investopedia.com/terms/t/tangibleasset.asp
https://www.wallstreetmojo.com/tangible-assets
https://www.nolo.com/legal-encyclopedia/free-books/small-business-book/chapter4-4.html
https://www.investopedia.com/what-happens-dont-pay-back-personal-loan-7555464
https://www.investopedia.com/terms/h/humancapital.asp
https://www.investopedia.com/terms/r/returnoninvestment.asp
https://corporatetraining.usf.edu/blog/continuing-education-as-an-investment-in-yourself
https://dariusforoux.com/education
https://www.investopedia.com/terms/l/loan.asp
https://www.wallstreetmojo.com/loan
https://www.youtube.com/watch?v=IZEzibhFClE
https://www.nerdwallet.com/article/loans/personal-loans/personal-loan-why-should-i-get
https://www.cnbc.com/select/questions-before-taking-out-personal-loan
https://www.getevolved.com/when-it-makes-sense-to-borrow-money
https://www.statefarm.com/simple-insights/financial/when-does-a-loan-make-sense
https://www.azquotes.com/quote/249566
https://www.gohenry.com/us/blog/financial-education/what-is-compound-interest-explaining-to-kids-and-teens
https://www.moneygeek.com/financial-planning/compound-interest-for-kids
https://www.ramseysolutions.com/retirement/how-teens-can-become-millionaires
https://www.visualcapitalist.com/cp/the-benefits-of-investing-early-in-life
https://www.investec.com/en_gb/wealth/our-offices/edinburgh/saving-early-and-often-the-benefits-of-compound-interest.html
https://www.nerdwallet.com/calculator/compound-interest-calculator
https://www.nerdwallet.com/article/investing/what-is-investing
https://www.easypeasyfinance.com/investing-for-kids-financial-literacy
https://www.forbes.com/sites/lizfrazierpeck/2023/02/01/why-teenagers-

should-start-investing-earlyand-3-proven-investment-tips-for-any-age/?sh=3a09213e70e0

https://www.axisbank.com/progress-with-us/invest/top-reasons-to-start-investing-at-an-early-age

https://www.willisowen.co.uk/help/long-term-benefits-investing

https://www.easypeasyfinance.com/investing-with-no-money-how-you-can-do-it

https://www.easypeasyfinance.com/risk-return-for-kids-beginners

https://www.nolafamily.com/financial-lessons-risk-vs-rewards

https://youngandtheinvested.com/investment-vehicles

https://www.nerdwallet.com/article/investing/types-of-investments

https://www.investopedia.com/terms/c/certificateofdeposit.asp

https://www.investopedia.com/ask/answers/012015/what-difference-between-reit-and-real-estate-fund.asp

https://www.investopedia.com/ask/answers/012015/what-difference-between-reit-and-real-estate-fund.asp

https://www.investopedia.com/ask/answers/100214/what-are-differences-between-investing-real-estate-and-stocks.asp

https://www.investopedia.com/terms/r/realestate.asp

https://www.thebalancemoney.com/real-estate-funds-vs-reits-5208631

https://www.investopedia.com/terms/c/collectible.asp

https://www.investopedia.com/articles/pf/08/fine-art.asp

https://www.investopedia.com/articles/basics/09/precious-metals-gold-silver-platinum.asp

https://www.bloomberg.com/news/newsletters/2022-03-18/is-jewelry-a-good-investment-yes-here-s-what-you-need-to-know

https://moneymade.io/learn/article/invest-in-classic-cars

https://tempuslogix.com/pros-and-cons-of-investing-in-classic-cars

https://www.themotorcyclebroker.co.uk/classic-motorcycle-investment-vs-classic-car-investment

https://www.vinovest.co/blog/investing-in-cars#link-1

https://www.nerdwallet.com/article/investing/cryptocurrency

https://www.nerdwallet.com/article/investing/nfts

https://decrypt.co/62898/most-expensive-nfts-ever-sold

https://www.investopedia.com/can-teenagers-invest-in-roth-iras-4770663

https://www.bankrate.com/retirement/custodial-roth-ira-starting-ira-for-your-child

https://www.investopedia.com/articles/personal-finance/110713/benefits-starting-ira-your-child.asp

https://money.com/teenagers-retirement-savings-roth-ira

https://www.nerdwallet.com/article/investing/diversification
https://www.investopedia.com/investing/importance-diversification
https://moneymade.io/learn/article/micro-investing-apps-for-your-kid
https://thisonlineworld.com/invest-10-and-earn-daily
https://www.goodreads.com/quotes/7119798-a-dream-written-down-with-a-date-becomes-a-goal
https://www.uopeople.edu/blog/dreams-vs-goals-the-differences-that-matter
https://planplusonline.com/whats-the-difference-between-a-goal-and-a-dream
https://timemanagementninja.com/2013/04/10-big-differences-between-goals-and-dreams-that-you-must-know
https://www.parents.com/parenting/better-parenting/teenagers/teen-talk/how-parents-can-help-their-teens-plan-for-the-future
https://www.nerdwallet.com/article/finance/financial-goals-definition-examples
https://hendershottwealth.com/e-mails/align-your-money-with-your-values
https://financeoverfifty.com/money-values
https://adebtfreestressfreelife.com/day-9-align-your-money-goals-and-values
https://www.self.com/story/values-based-financial-goals
https://danielkarim.com/how-to-turn-your-dreams-into-goals-the-s-m-a-r-t-goal-setting-model
https://hellogiggles.com/ways-celebrate-an-accomplishment-dont-involve-money
https://thefrugalite.com/treat-yourself-without-spending-money
https://www.happierhuman.com/money-affirmations
https://blog.gratefulness.me/money-affirmations
https://www.brightspacecoaching.com/blog/60-abundance-affirmations-money-affirmations
https://www.moneyforthemamas.com/money-affirmations

Made in United States
Orlando, FL
14 December 2024